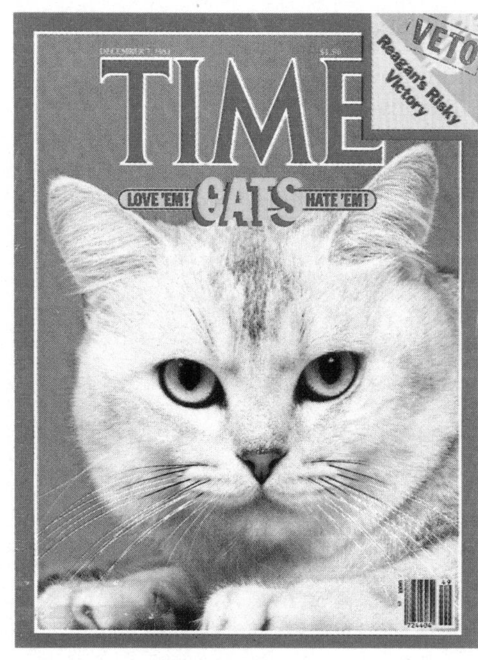


**"CATS, LOVE 'EM OR HATE 'EM, ARE A HOT NUMBER... THEY ARE BECOMING A NATIONAL MANIA. IN FACT, CATS ARE EVEN GAINING ON DOGS."—*TIME***

When our cat, Leilah, read those words from *Time* magazine's cover story about the ongoing cat craze, she said, "So cats are In. So what else is mew?"

As any cat can tell you, cats have never been Out. *Felis catus* has been stirring the human imagination for thousands of years. Ancient Egypt worshipped the cat as a god; Medieval Europe feared it as demonic. Either way, we'd call that being In, really In! Every catfoot of the way, talented folk have fashioned the feline's graceful, playful, seductive and mysterious images out of everything from paint to porcelain to precious metals and gems. That fascination with cats, and the creativity it inspires, have never been as lively, as large scale, as right now.

Contemporary America has been given the long tale of the cat a new twist: the cat as Big Business. Cat food sales and cat care services and products are now major industries. Cat-design merchandise for people finds a hugely responsive market. Much of this market is reached via mail-order.

The familiar images of Felix, Garfield, Morris, Heathcliff and Kliban Cats, decorating everything from calendars to coffee mugs, represent only a small part of the merchandise available for cat lovers and for cats themselves. The tip of the catberg, we might say (and will!).

Personally, we find this cornucopia of caterphernalia surprising,

entertaining, even useful. We thought you might, too—hence, this book. What you'll discover in these pages is a mere sampling of the thousands of cat-related items currently being offered by catalog houses, museums, shops, individual artists and craftsmen, and others. While many of the items can be purchased directly from the purveyor, and some not, all can be purchased by mail or phone, after preliminary inquiry.

*How to inquire about, or order the merchandise shown:* THE MAIL-ORDER CAT is a source book, not a catalog. You cannot order directly from it. If, however, while browsing you see an item you'd like to own or give as a gift, note the code letter and number given at or near the end of the item's description. (Example: 125-C) The number is keyed to the Source List at the end of the book, which tells you where to write or phone for availability and ordering information. The letter indicates the price range, and an explanation of this is to be found with the Source List as well. These details are, of course, subject to change.

A word about another special power of cats: cats frequently cause otherwise sensible humans to make terrible puns. (Example: "a purrr-fect gift.") Since every item in this book really *is* purrr-fect, we decided to resist the cat's power with all our strength. We decided the best way would be to get it out of our system, all at once, in this introduction. In our descriptive text, we have stuck to the facts—and not one word fur-ther.

Welcome to the pick of the litter!

LARGE EGYPTIAN CAT, page 122.

GARFIELD in plush, with felt top hat, satiny bow tie and red rose. 9½" H. (868620) 8PS-B

KITTY KABANA™ covers the litter box. Attractive anywhere. Gives the cat the privacy it likes. Designed for convenient litter changes. Easy to assemble metal frame covered with machine washable fabric coverlet, available in a variety of styles and colors. Fits standard litter pan sizes up to 19½"Lx15½"W. Assembled dimensions: 20"Lx16"Wx22"H at the apex. 132-C. A companion bed is available; also additional covers which fit either frame (bed or litter box).

4

BOOKENDS go gracefully up and over. In hand painted wood. (J569384) 8NH-B

LIMITED EDITION SERIES of four fine china plates uses no less than 23 shades of color to picture their feline subjects. Hand applied 24K gold rims. Signed and numbered by the artist, with certificate of authenticity. I: The Baron (J86806) 8PS-F. II: Her Majesty (J868075) 8PS-F. III. The Dutchess (J868083) 8PS-F. IV: His Lordship (J868091) 8PS-F. 4-Plate Set (J868109) 8PS-K

SCHERENSCHNITTE. Circle of playful black cats is cut from single piece of paper. The work of Blanch Turner, each is signed, framed in oak and ready to hang. 9½"x7½". (8407) 57-D

WE DON'T WANT YOU TO SMOKE.
YOUR FURRY FRIENDS DON'T WANT YOU TO SMOKE. YOUR LUNG ASSOCIATION DOESN'T WANT YOU TO SMOKE. THAT'S WHY THIS POSTER WAS CREATED. WE PLACED IT HERE BECAUSE WE DON'T WANT YOU TO SMOKE EITHER. ESPECIALLY HERE.

"WE DON'T WANT YOU TO SMOKE." Poster by artist Braldt Bralds. 40-B

BLANKET CATS by Jan Farley are made from vintage army blankets and coats. 16-B

SNUFF THE CAT & FLUFF are brightly painted boxes by The Friends. Large: 16-G, Small: 16-B

"FOLK CAT WITH YARN" Bold-colored handmade rug. Designed by Miki Kaplan; made by Pat Nolen. 24"x30". 16-L

"KITTY, KITTY." Hooked rug based on a traditional design. Handmade by Pat Hornafius. 17"x27". 16-L

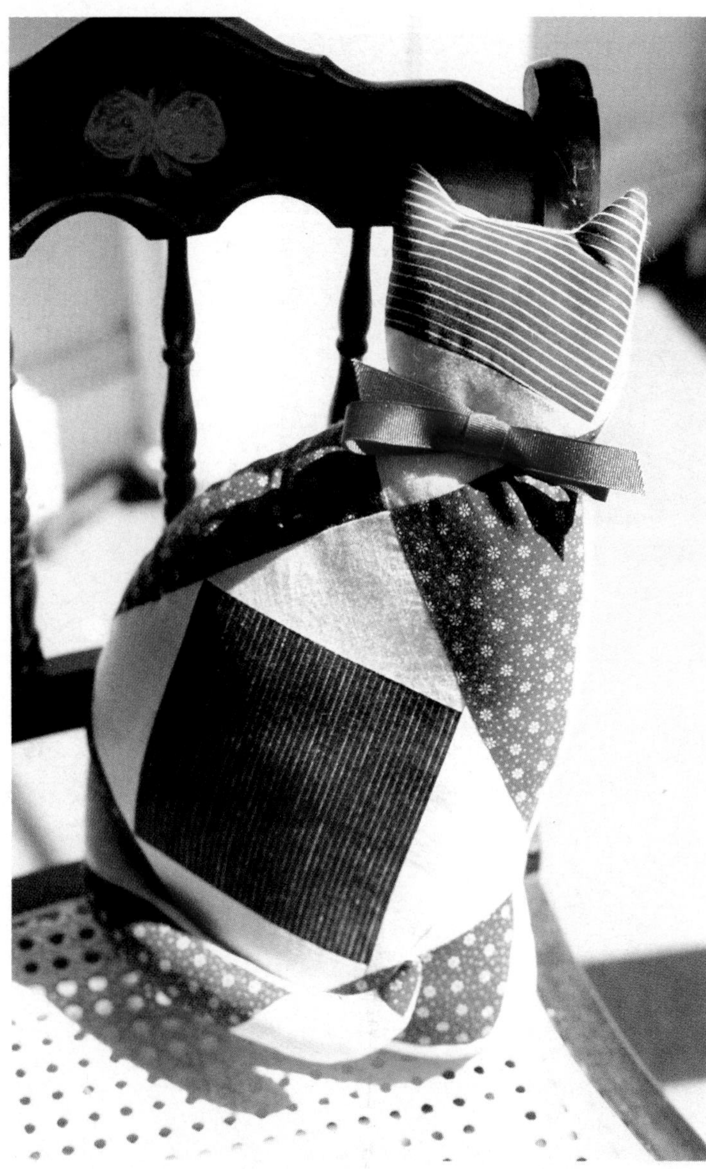

DOORSTOP CAT by Shirley Over is fashioned of old quilts and tied with a bright ribbon. Approx. 15″ high. 16-E

WOODEN TRINKET BOXES are stenciled by artist Gail Owen. May be used to store small things, as gift boxes, or as gifts themselves. 16-B

CAT CRITTERS by Susan Miller are made from old quilts. May be used as Christmas ornaments or pin cushions. 16-B

EDWARDIAN CAT FAMILY. Printed in England, these are available in kit form or as finished dolls. Left to right: Puss-in-Boots, 15″ high. Stuffed, 52-B. Kit, 52-A. Master Timothy Cat, 10″ high. Stuffed, 52-A. Kit, 52-A. Mrs. Clara Cat, 15″ high. Stuffed, 52-B. Kit, 52-A. Mr. Thomas Cat, 15″ high. Stuffed, 52-B. Kit, 52-A. Miss Kitty Cat, 10″ high. Stuffed, 52-A. Kit, 52-A.

HANDWOVEN RUG from India is of pure cotton. Printed black cats on woven stripes of cream, light blue and mauve. 4x6 feet. (DM992) 98-H

PORCELAIN SCULPTURE of cat with person's face mask. Hand crafted and hand painted. 2½″ high. (LM898A) 98-C

"FAT CAT" is crafted in terra cotta. It is hollow, yet heavy enough to be a doorstop. 9"Lx11"Hx8"W. (N462) 98-D

NEST OF FOUR BOXES. Graduated tin boxes,each topped with a cat illustration. Smallest is 4" square x 2" high; largest is 7" square x 3½" high. (BM987) 98-C

SIAMESE WITH BLUE EYES. Of hand cast stone medium with glass eyes and felt base. 7" long. (XM466) 98-D

HELLO KITTY
HELLO KITTY
K

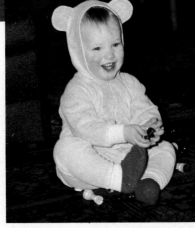

CAT & MOUSE PLAYSUITS. Dramatic black and white velour cat, for Halloween or any party. Add a hat with plume and high boots and you have "Puss 'n Boots." The mouse is soft gray velour with pink. For sizes to fit children from 6-12 months of age to 6-8 years. 59D-E

"HELLO KITTY" sheet set. Complete set includes1 twin flat sheet, 1 twin fitted, 1 standard pillow case. 65% polyester, 35% cotton. Machine washable, no iron. 13-C; matching comforter and coordinated terry bath towels and washcloths are also available. © 1976 Sanrio Co., Ltd.

PLAYFUL FIGURINES for shelf or table, or in with plants. Hand painted bisque porcelain. (G754143) Set of 3, 8MW-A

STRAWBERRY CAT DOORSTOP curls cozily on the floor. Handcut from wood in a two-dimensional design. Hand painted and signed by the artist. 14"Lx7"H. 9C

THE KIT CAT KLOCK is a classic. Animated electric clock features rolling eyes and wagging tail. Overall size 15½"x4", in assorted colors. Plain Kit Cat (C-1), 23-D; jeweled Kit Cat, facing page (JC-1), 23-E

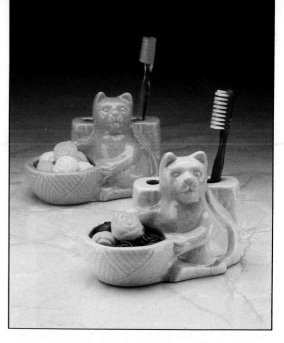

SOAP AND TOOTHBRUSH DISH. The soap dish looks like the cat's ball of yarn. Highly glazed ceramic in gray, rust or blue. (G678136B) 8NH-A

PATCHWORK KITTEN made from an old quilt by Holly Horton. 16-B

CAT AND CANARY MUSICAL CERAMIC. The canary moves in and out of reach of the cat's paw while the full chorus of "I Will Wait For You" plays on. Approx. 6"H (G679662) 8NH-B

"HAUTE FELINE." Gourmet fish snack for cats. Baked into small, crunchy, fish-shaped biscuits. 24 oz. jar. (G793596)8-B; 10 oz. bag. (G794446) 8HA-A

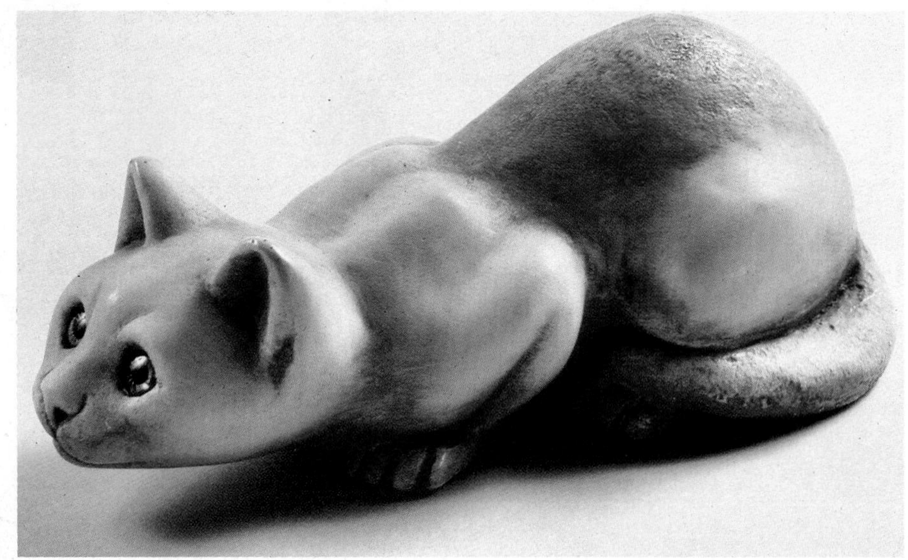

CROUCHING SIAMESE for fireside or windowsill, or to stop a door. Bisque-finish durastone with blue, blue eyes. 9¼″ (G518449) 8OV-B

GRIZABELLA MUSICAL FIGURINE plays "Memory," her haunting theme song. Porcelain. 7" high. 73-D

"CATS." A 2-record album of the popular musical, with music by Andrew Lloyd Webber and text based on T.S. Eliot's "Old Possum's Book of Practical Cats." Issued by Geffen Records. 10-B

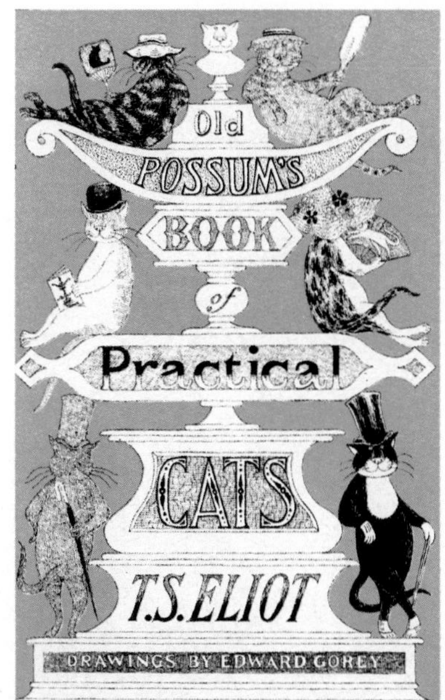


"OLD POSSUM'S BOOK OF PRACTICAL CATS" by T.S. Eliot is the book of poems that inspired the hit show "Cats." This paperback edition is illustrated by Edward Gorey. $5\frac{3}{8}$"x8"; 48 pages. 69-A

MUSIC BOXES. Both play "Memory." Round box 4" diameter; covered box $4\frac{1}{2}$"x$3\frac{1}{2}$". Each, 73-B

CAT COLLECTORS © is an international club of cat enthusiasts. Members enjoy collecting cat-related quality art, antiques, books, jewelry, and items such as the ones from the Broadway hit show, "CATS," shown here. A bi-monthly newsletter, CAT TALK ©, is sent to members. For information, please see Source List. All "Cats" items: © Roman, Inc. ™ © 1981 The Really Useful Company, Limited.

"CATS" TINS, featuring the show's most memorable characters. Three nestled tins, the largest 5" high. 73-A

GRIZABELLA PLATE. Limited Edition. 8½" diameter. 73-B

UNICEF'S "KRUMEICH CATS." Cards designed by U.S. artist/illustrator Thaddeus Krumeich. Printed on high-gloss paper; accompanying blue envelopes are made from recycled paper. Notes only, no greetings. Card size 4⅜"x6⅛". Pack of 10, 2 of each design, with envelopes. (83507n) 105-A

"CROCHETED CATS AND KITTENS." Twenty-three designs for toys, pillows, wall hangings and other projects by Barbara and Ruth Jacksier. Drawings, charts, and complete directions. 95-A

"THE CAT COLORING BOOK" by Karen Baldauski has information on the breeds shown, and instructions for correct coloring. 95-A

IRON-ON TRANSFER PATTERNS. Eighty-eight images of cats and kittens by artist Janette Aiello may be used for embroidery, woodburning, appliqué projects and more. Complete directions. 95-A

POSTCARDS. Twenty-four ready-to-mail postcards feature full color photographs of cats and kittens by Dorothy Holby. 95-A

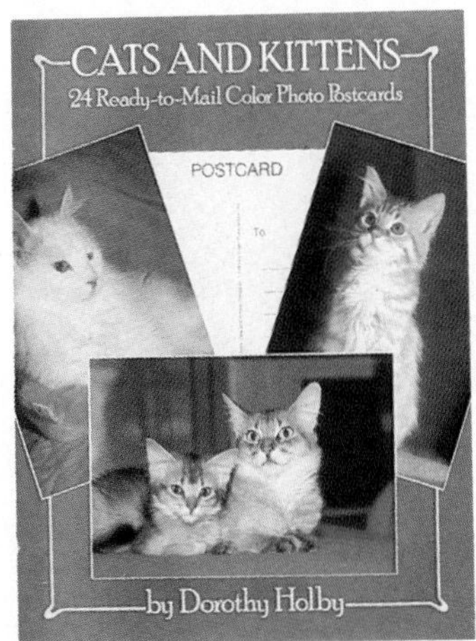

CAT PORTRAIT DOLLS. These dolls are created by Richard Palan from photos of your cat, and use your suggestions for costume. The dolls are 15" tall, have painted and glazed heads, are stuffed and then extravagantly costumed with fine fabrics, bits of antique lace, fur, ribbons, jewels, etc. 1-K to L

THE WHITE CAT FAMILY

RED TABBY CAT DOLL

SANTA CAT DOLL

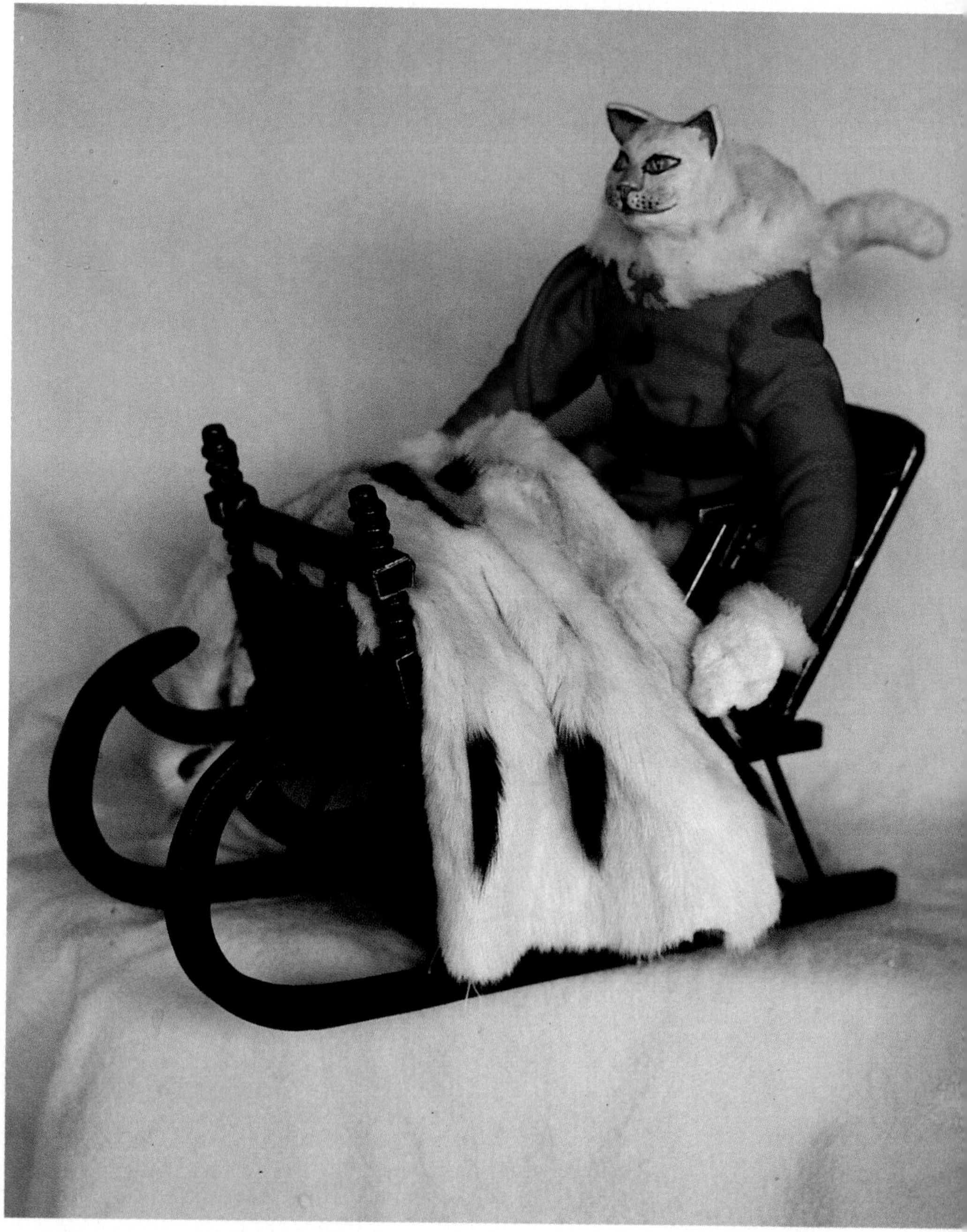

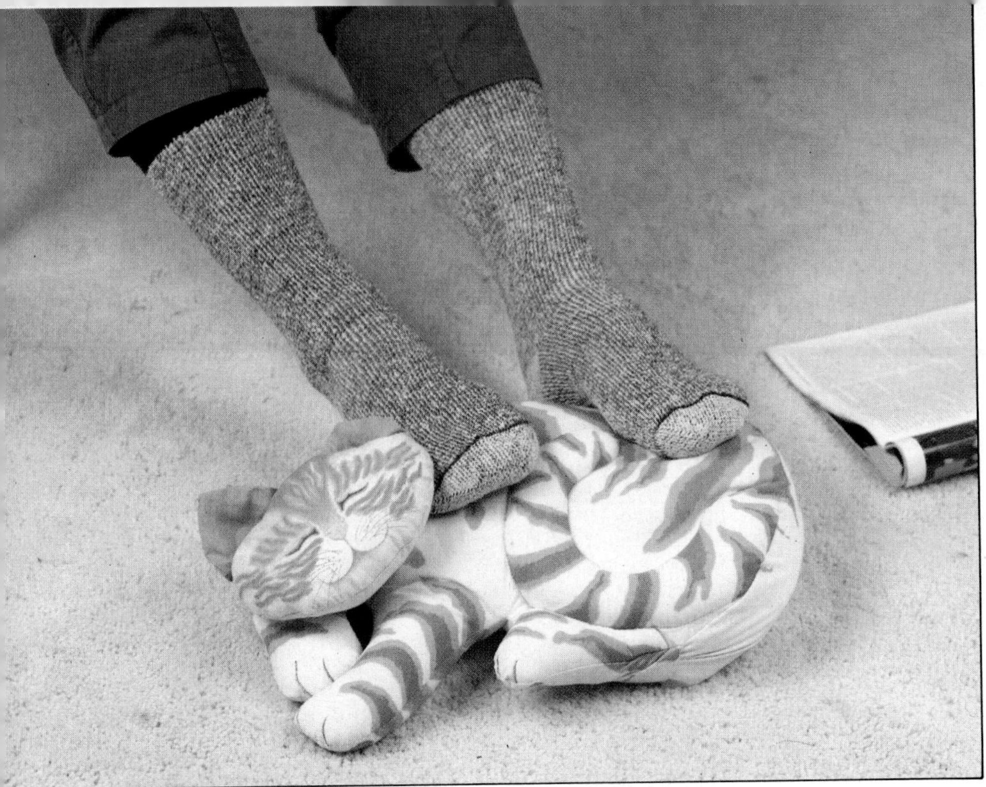

FOOT MASSAGER. Tabby "purrs" under pressure from a foot and the vibrations soothe tired feet. Works for back muscles too. Of silk screened muslin, 16" long. Batteries not included. (79373) 58PP-D

NEEDLEPOINT CHINA CAT. Stitch a picture of pillow top. Kit includes design hand painted on 13-mesh canvas, Persian yarns, needle and instructions. 14"x12" (618973) 58S-D

VEST AND PURSE. By Terrie Milestone Soldavini in 100% cotton quilted with polyester batting fiberfill. Preshrunk, washable. Reversible vest in sizes for ages 3 to 9 (174) 24-C; Purse, shoulder bag or clutch, fully lined, washable (175) 24-B; the set (175a) 24-E

WASTE PAPER BIN in metal, with laminated print. 8½"x13". (79183) 58PP-C

SIAMESE SILHOUETTE to stitch in cross stitch and other basic embroidery stitches. Design by Julie Shearer. Kit includes design stamped on white homespun, and all other needs. 12″x12″. (503693) 58S-B; 12″x12″ wooden frame. (962483) 58S-B

KITCHEN TILES NEEDLEPOINT DESIGN by Susan Marie McChesney to stitch yourself. ''No Matter What'' kit includes all materials and instructions. 14″x14″. (113013) 58S-B

CROSS STITCH MOTTO. Stitch-it-yourself kit includes design stamped on white homespun, and all else, including wooden frame. 8″x10″. (014773) 58S-B

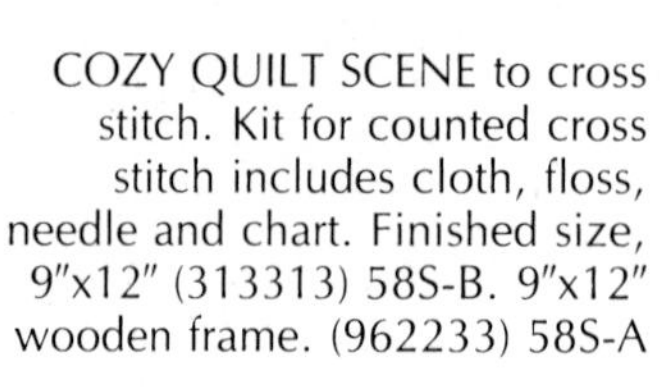

COZY QUILT SCENE to cross stitch. Kit for counted cross stitch includes cloth, floss, needle and chart. Finished size, 9″x12″ (313313) 58S-B. 9″x12″ wooden frame. (962233) 58S-A

''CAT-A-LONG'' pull toy. Solid pine, non-toxic paint. (176) 24-C. All part of The Cat Companion Collection.™

HAND BURNISHED BRASS. Highly detailed chokers and matching earrings. Seated cat choker. (C327) 62-B; Seated cat earrings. (C327) 62-B; Cat head choker. (C283) 62-B; Cat head earrings. (C283) 62-B.

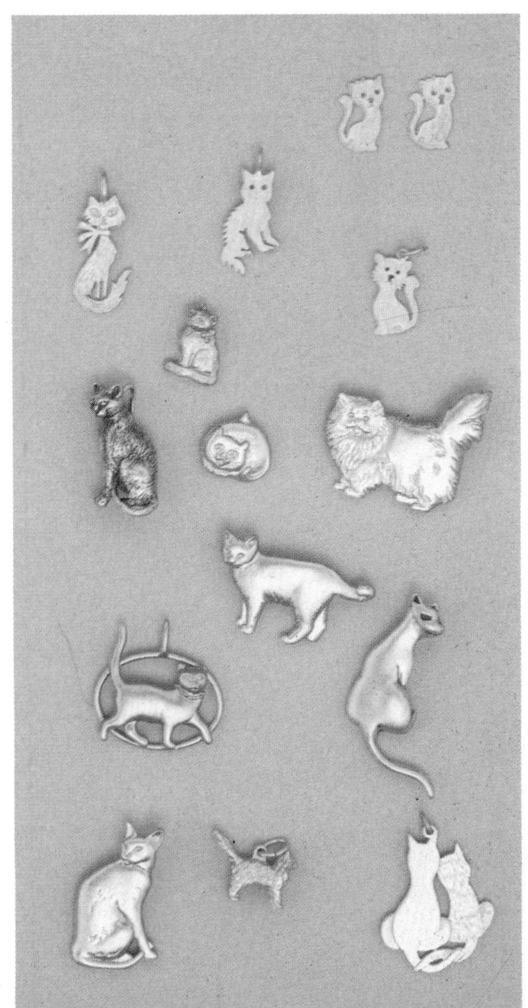

CATS GALORE. Earrings, pendants, charms and lapel pins. All available in silver and many in vermeil or 14K. 62-B to 62-L.

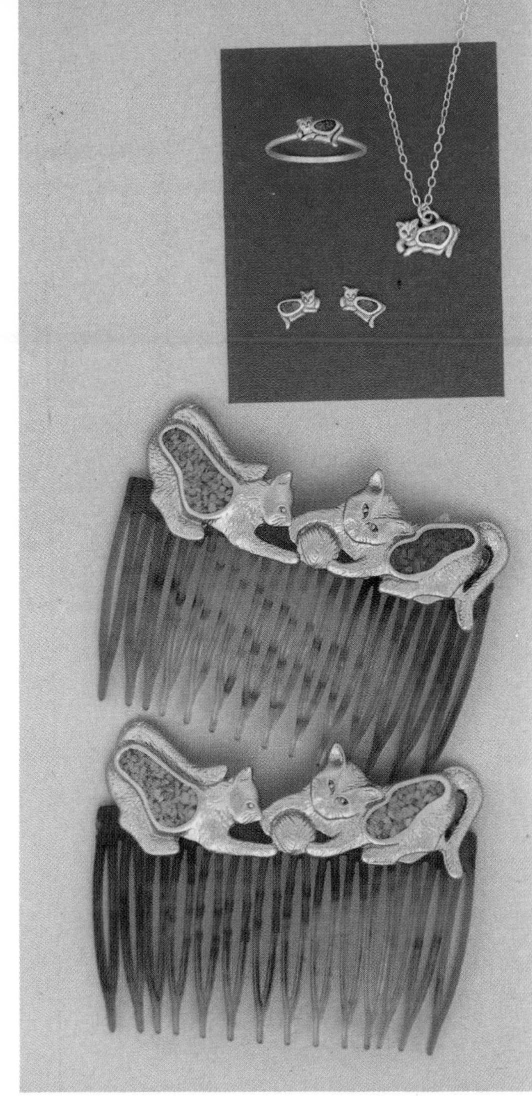

WESTERN STYLE JEWELERY in silver with genuine turquoise and coral from New Mexico. Silver and turquoise cat ring. (R841) 62-A; Silver and turquoise pendant. (N743) 62-A; Haircomb with coral. (W351C) 62-B, pair 62-C; Haircomb with turquoise. (W351T) 62-B, pair 62-C.

HAND ENAMELED BRASS PENDANT. (P321) 62-B

POLISHED BRASS LAPEL PIN. (56) 62-A

HAND CRAFTED CLOISONNE post earrings. (4341) 62-B

ENAMELED CAT CHARMS in assorted colors. (C128) 62-A

SCATTER PINS. Hand enameled in black or lavender. (310041) 62-C

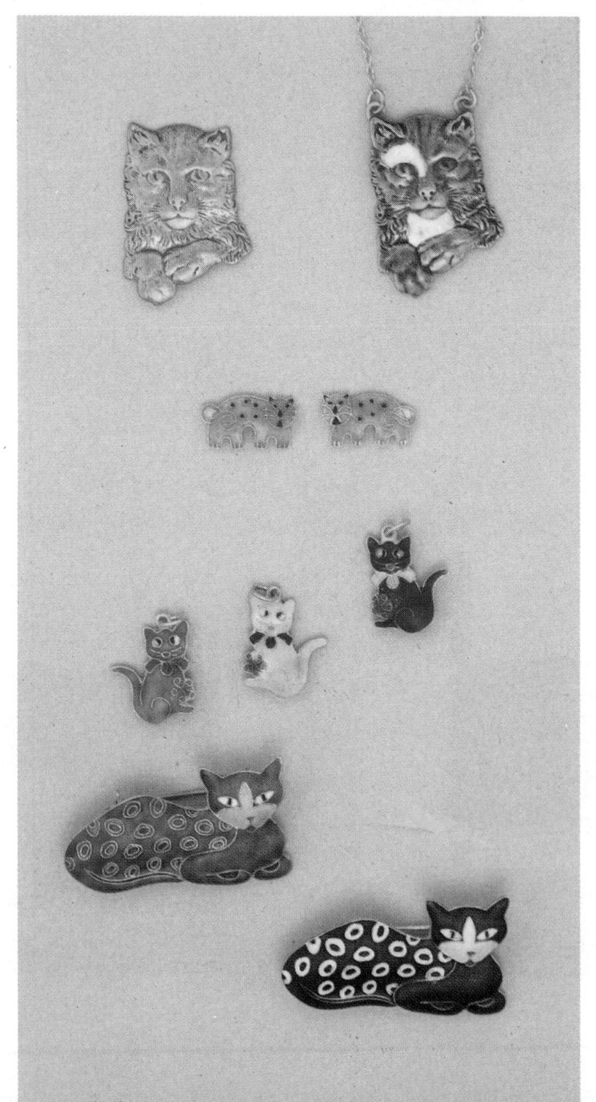

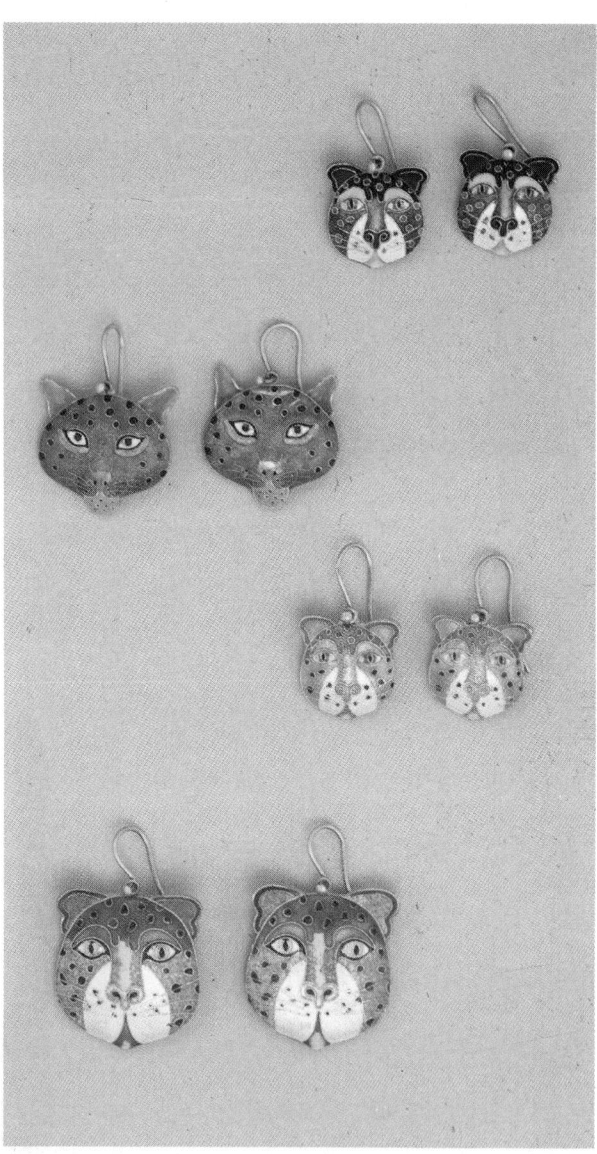

COLORFUL CLOISONNE earrings are hand enameled and each pair is meticulously matched. Dark blue cat earrings. (5511B) 62-C; Jaguar earrings. (5951) 62-B; Light blue cat earrings. (5511T) 62-C; Jumbo cat earrings. (5521) 62-B.

SOLID LEAD CRYSTAL. "Perky," imported from Italy. Bright metal nose and whiskers, black eyes, and when you turn him around—surprise! A graceful tail curves up his back. 3½" on 1" base. (169) 24-B. Part of The Cat Companion Collection™.

SERVING TRAYS. Elizabeth Brownd designs. Lovely on the wall when not in use. Wooden trays have stain-resistant print inserts. Each, 21″x14¾″.(30263, peonies), (30253, irises) 58PP-C

MUSICAL FIGURINE plays "Pussycat, Pussycay." Hand decorated ceramic. 6″H. (G678730) 8NH-A

CAST IRON BOOKENDS. Cat is split in the middle, one half for each end. Heavy bases stay put. (G57197G) 8HH-B

FINE GLAZED EARTHENWARE MUGS. Cobalt blue. 12 oz. size, 3¾" tall. (G819896) Singly or pair, 8OV-A

"CHESSIE© Sleep like a Kitten Golden Anniversary Plate." Eight-inch, fine porcelain, with gold edge. A railroad authorized Limited Edition, numbered; with commemorative message. Gift boxes. 138-C

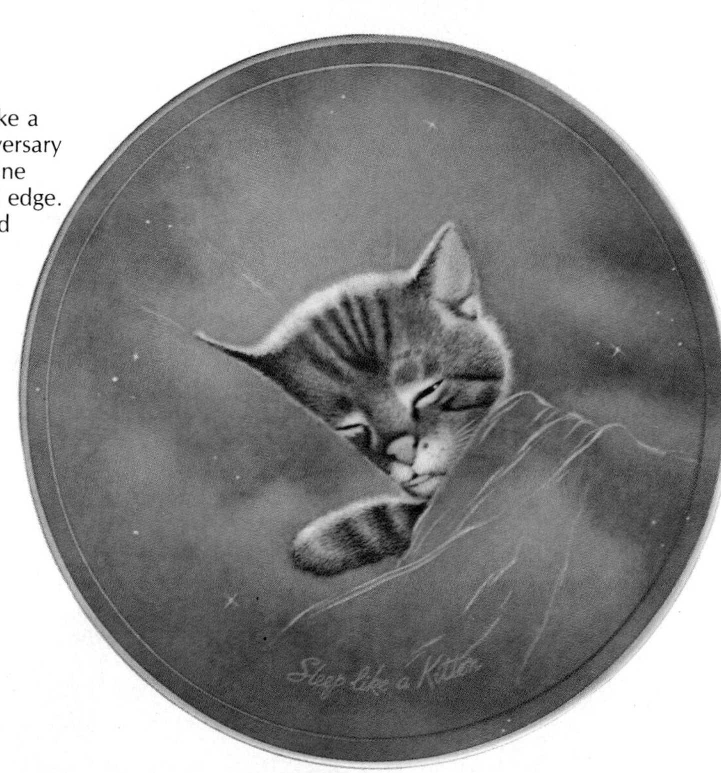


NESTING TINS. Use them for cookies or candy; as gifts, individually or as a set. They nest together for neat storage. (G563973) Set of 4, 8OV-A

Moses the Kitten

James Herriot

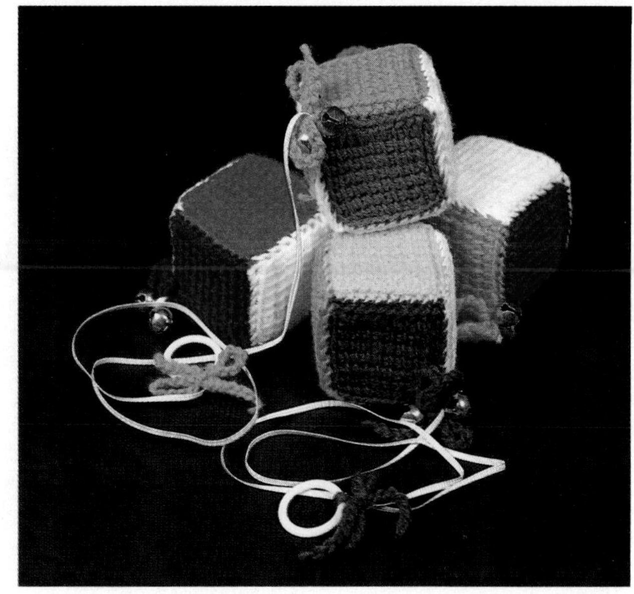

KITTY BLOCKS. Hand crocheted by Aunt Velma and filled with fresh catnip. Elastic pull string. 75-A

COOKIE CUTTER with wooden box. The cat face is 3½″x3½″. Box stores the cutter. The set, 75-A

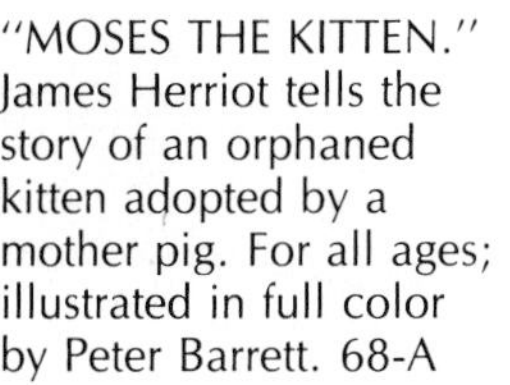

"MOSES THE KITTEN." James Herriot tells the story of an orphaned kitten adopted by a mother pig. For all ages; illustrated in full color by Peter Barrett. 68-A

"SAMURAI CAT." Set in sixteenth-century Japan, our hero, Miaowara Tomokata, is on a mission of vengeance and tomfoolery. Full-color paintings plus black and white illustrations. 94-A

BUMPER STICKER. Available free.
See source List no. 75 for instructions.

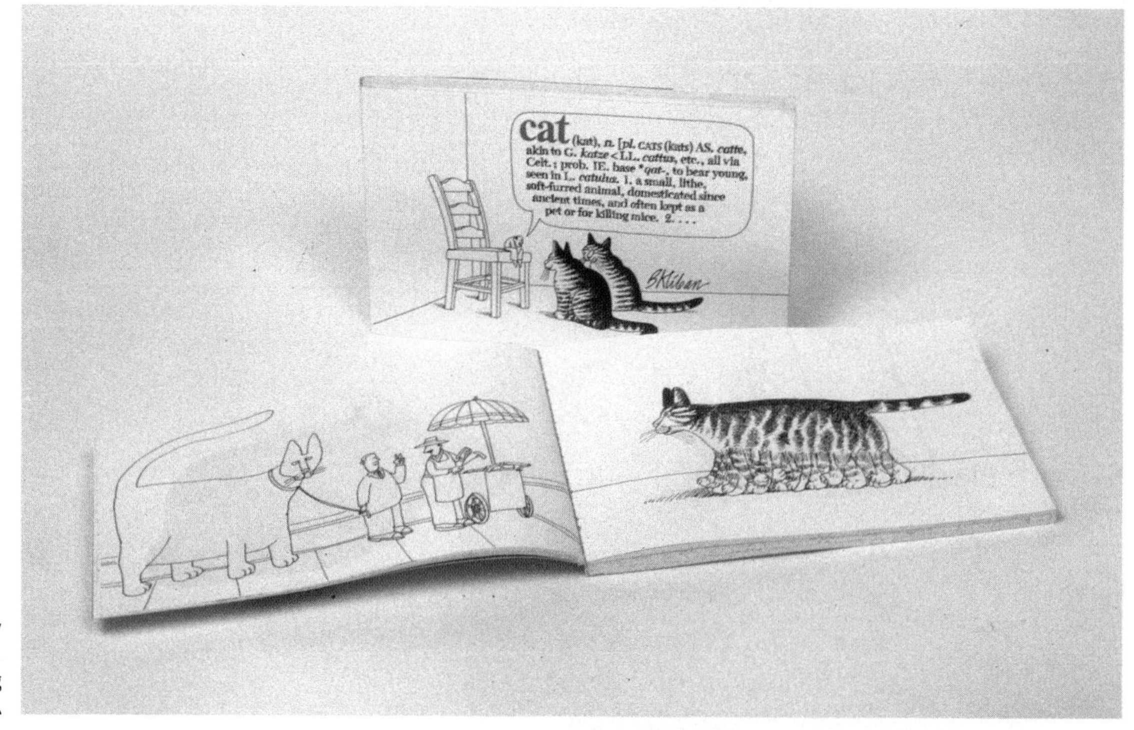


"CAT" by B. Kliban. This latter-day classic has sold nearly a million copies. It's the book that gave new meaning to "wacka wacka." © 1975 B.Kliban. 3-A

DOUBLE LONG-HAIRED CATS. An exclusive design appliqued on fashion-colored pullover sweatshirts of 50% cotton/50% acrilan. Design suitable for large sizes only. © 1984 Marjory Warren, NY, NY 6-H

MIMI VANG OLSEN is perhaps the best-known portrait painter of cats working today. When she is given a commission, she insists on visiting and spending time with the cat or cats to be pictured. She explores the personality and habits of each animal, makes many photographic studies, and is only then ready to begin work on each very individual cat portrait. She works in oil on canvas and her prices are based on the number of cats to be pictured. Shown here are four of her paintings which suggest something of their variety. 108-O

©Mimi Vang Olsen

PLUSH FELIX THE CAT. 15″ high. (DP7392) 25-B. Felix Painter's Cap. (DP7089) 25-A. © 1983 Felix the Cat Productions, King Features Syndicate.

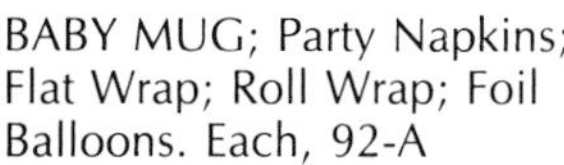

BABY MUG; Party Napkins; Flat Wrap; Roll Wrap; Foil Balloons. Each, 92-A

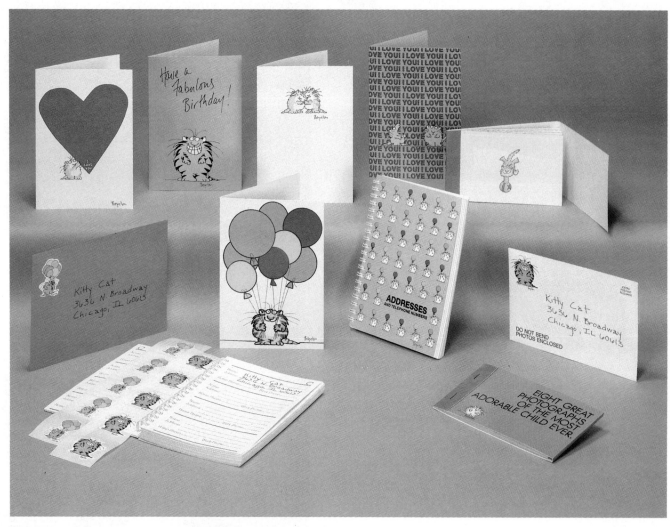

PHOTOMAILER; Address Book; Stickers; Cards. Each, 92-A

CERAMIC CAT HOOKS. Black and white (CA 402) or Siamese (CA 403). Each, 25-B

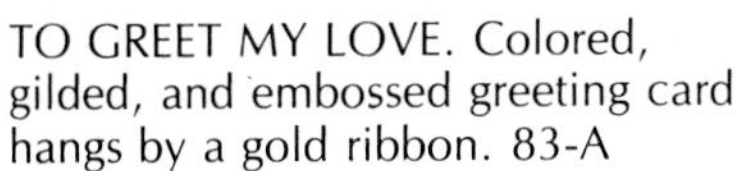

TO GREET MY LOVE. Colored, gilded, and embossed greeting card hangs by a gold ribbon. 83-A

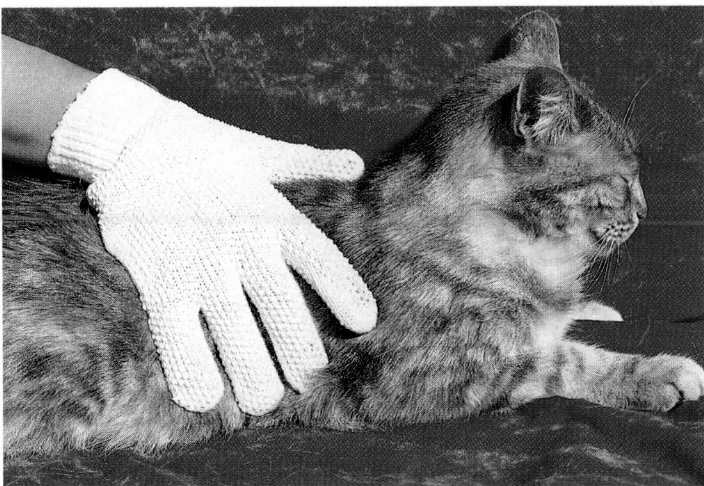

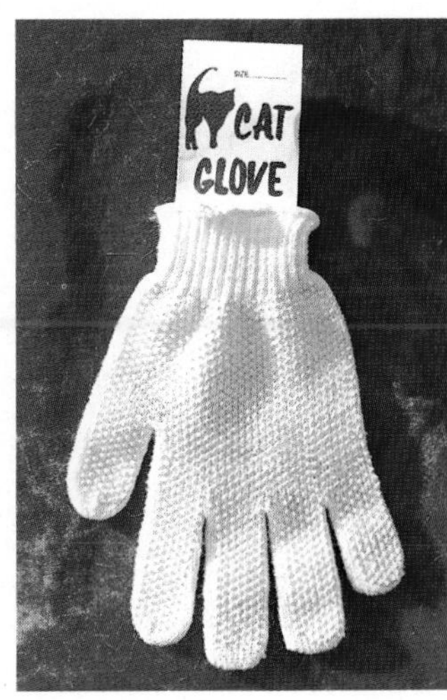


CAT GLOVE. Hundreds of delicate nodules gently lift and hold shedding fur as you stroke your pet. This washable grooming glove leaves your cat shiny and contented. Specify men's or women's. 30-A

GREETINGS that become 3-dimensional sculptures. Hand silk-screened on heavyweight stock, precisely cut, ready to assemble. Each with an envelope and a blank notecard for personal message. (G989830) Set of 2, 8AY-A

TOOTHPICKS, SALT AND PEPPER are served by these three ceramic kittens. Shakers 3″ high, holder 2½″ high. (G56612). Set of 3, 8HH-A

ANGLED SCRATCHING POST, designed for the ideal scratching position. Cats can also scratch on the base or scratch upside down or under the post with their hind legs. Fine quality short nap carpeting in neutral colors. Shades of browns and greys; special color requests considered. Base 20″x20″x1″. Post 30″x2″x4″. 101-D

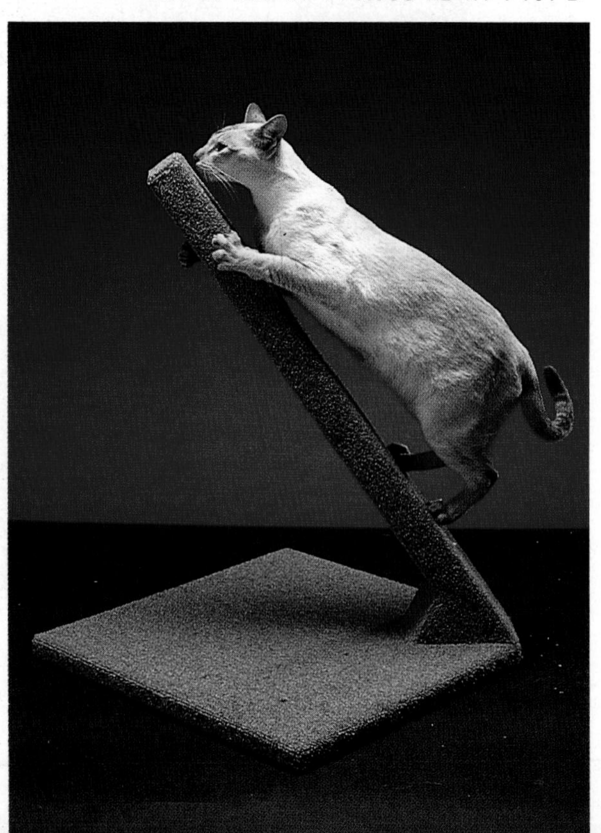

ZELLER SCHWARZE KATZ. Light white wines imported by Leonard Kreusch, Inc. 19-A

REAL POSTAGE STAMPS for collectors interested in specific topics. A starter collection of topical stamps (in this instance, cats) can be had for about a dollar. Along with it is included other sets of cat stamps, foreign and domestic, which you can examine and purchase, or return without obligation. 12-A

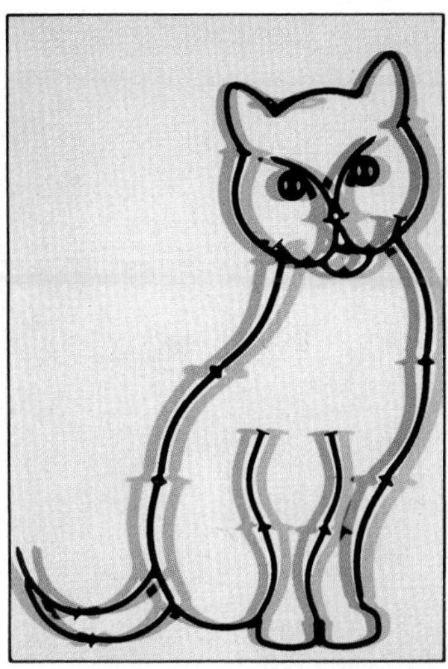

CAT SCULPTURE.
Hand crafted metal.
Approx. 8½″ tall. 32-A

CAT SCULPTURE.
Hand crafted metal.
Approx. 3½″ tall. 32-A

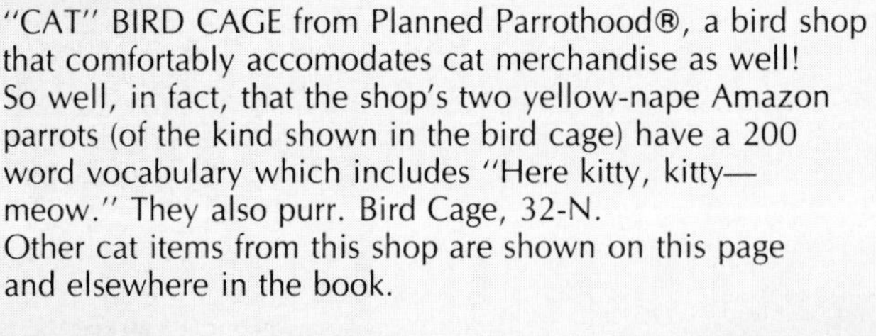

"CAT" BIRD CAGE from Planned Parrothood®, a bird shop that comfortably accomodates cat merchandise as well! So well, in fact, that the shop's two yellow-nape Amazon parrots (of the kind shown in the bird cage) have a 200 word vocabulary which includes "Here kitty, kitty—meow." They also purr. Bird Cage, 32-N.
Other cat items from this shop are shown on this page and elsewhere in the book.

PEWTER KEYCHAINS. Designed and signed by the artist. Available in many different cat breeds. 32-A

TUXEDO CAT. Exclusive design is appliquéd on a selection of fashion-colored pullover sweatshirts made of 50%cotton and 50% acrilan. Machine washable. Sizes S-M-L © 1984 Marjory Warren, NY, NY 6-E

CAT FACE. An exclusive design appliquéed on a selection of fashion-colored pullover sweatshirts, 50% cotton/50% acrilan. S-M-L. Machine washable. © 1984 Marjory Warren, NY, NY 6-E

SIAMESE CAT CUSHION. 15″ square cushion cover with 2″ sham border. Envelope back opening for easy removal. Muslin covered pillow insert included. © 1984 Marjory Warren, NY, NY

TUXEDO CAT CUSHION. With 13″x17″ tailored edge cover. Envelope back opening for easy removal Muslin covered pillow insert included. © 1984 Marjory Warren, NY, NY. 6-E

VIENNA BRONZES. Four lively figures for the collector or gift giver. Cat and Mouse (E737VB) 88-K. Rain Cat on Cushion (E717VB) 88-K. Sledding Cat (E746VB) 88-K. Scaredy-Cat (E877VB) 88-K

"ORVIS DOG'S NEST®" IS FOR CATS TOO. Poly/cotton twill denim cover zips off for washing. Inside is a second layer of sturdy fabric to contain bed material that retains animal's body heat but won't take on animal odors. Use the nest for back of car or anywhere you need it. Kids love it too. Royal Stewart Tartan (#78), Blue Denim (#76), Hunting Green (#80), and Orvis Logo pattern (#77). Nests range in size for pets under 15 lbs. to 60 lbs. and over, 26" to 45". 76-C to 76-E. Extra covers available.

VALENTINE CAT of porcelain. Hand sculpted, hand painted, signed and dated. An exclusive design. Approx. 2" high (each varies slightly). (N458) 98-D

ORIGINAL SIGNED POTTERY
by Carlyle Tiegland.

"WHIMSICAL CAT" mug is handmade and holds a generous 10 ounces. Brown only. 34-B.

"WHIMSICAL CAT" footed bowl is handmade and may be used as a pet dish, or to hold soap, sponges, etc. Brown only. 34-B.

"WHIMSICAL CAT" lamp is handmade and approximately 10" tall. Its sturdy base makes it good for a child's room. Brown only. Shade not included. 34-E.

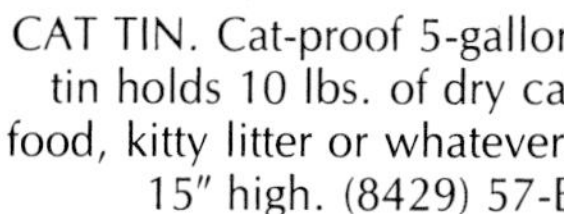

CAT TIN. Cat-proof 5-gallon tin holds 10 lbs. of dry cat food, kitty litter or whatever. 15" high. (8429) 57-B

"BAD CATS." In 60 wickedly humorous drawings, artist Sami Lais shreds the myth of the placid, charming cat on the hearth, and exposes the *real* feline obsessions. 68-B

HOT WATER BOTTLE COVER. Hand silk-screened on polyester and cotton, with quilted interior. 10″x15″. Snaps over a standard hot water bottle (not included). (F480Q) 88-B

FAMILY OF DRAFT DODGERS. Mama cat and her kittens, evenly stuffed and weighted to fit snugly across drafty windows or doors, help prevent costly heat leaks. Use also as fun pillow or room decoration. Hand screened muslin, 39″Lx10″H. 9-C

PLANTER. Fashioned after an Early American design. Hand decorated fine ceramic. 7½"H, 4⅝"W. (G678870) 8NH-B

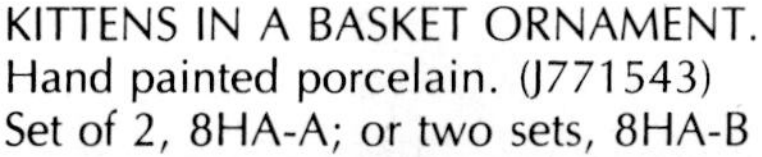

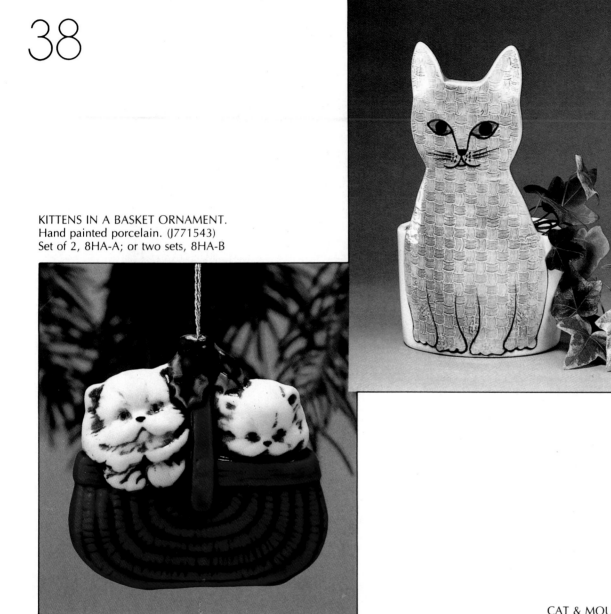

KITTENS IN A BASKET ORNAMENT. Hand painted porcelain. (J771543) Set of 2, 8HA-A; or two sets, 8HA-B

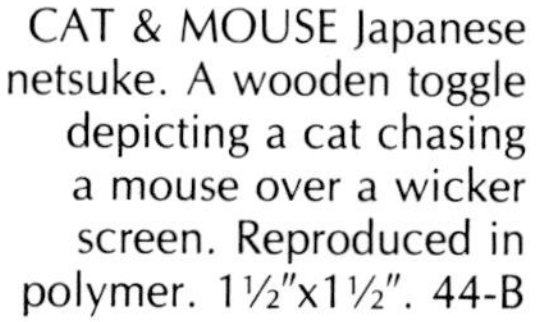

CAT & MOUSE Japanese netsuke. A wooden toggle depicting a cat chasing a mouse over a wicker screen. Reproduced in polymer. 1½"x1½". 44-B

MIRRORED SCULPTURE, hand cast and colored. Of fine gypsum materials, special paints and stains. Mirror is 9" diameter. (G679779) 8NH-B

CAT COASTERS. Pastel and gold full-color coasters are cork-backed and alcohol-proof. Boxed set of six. (8417) 57-B

COCKTAIL NAPKINS are Pam Marker's adaptations from the Collections of The Metropolitan Museum of Art. The boxed set of facial quality tissue includes fifty each of four designs. (38623) 58PP-B

DRAFT-BLOCKER for windows and doors can also curl up as a door stop. Cotton/polyester stuffed with sand. 36" long. Blue or pink (G904045B) 8TAP-A

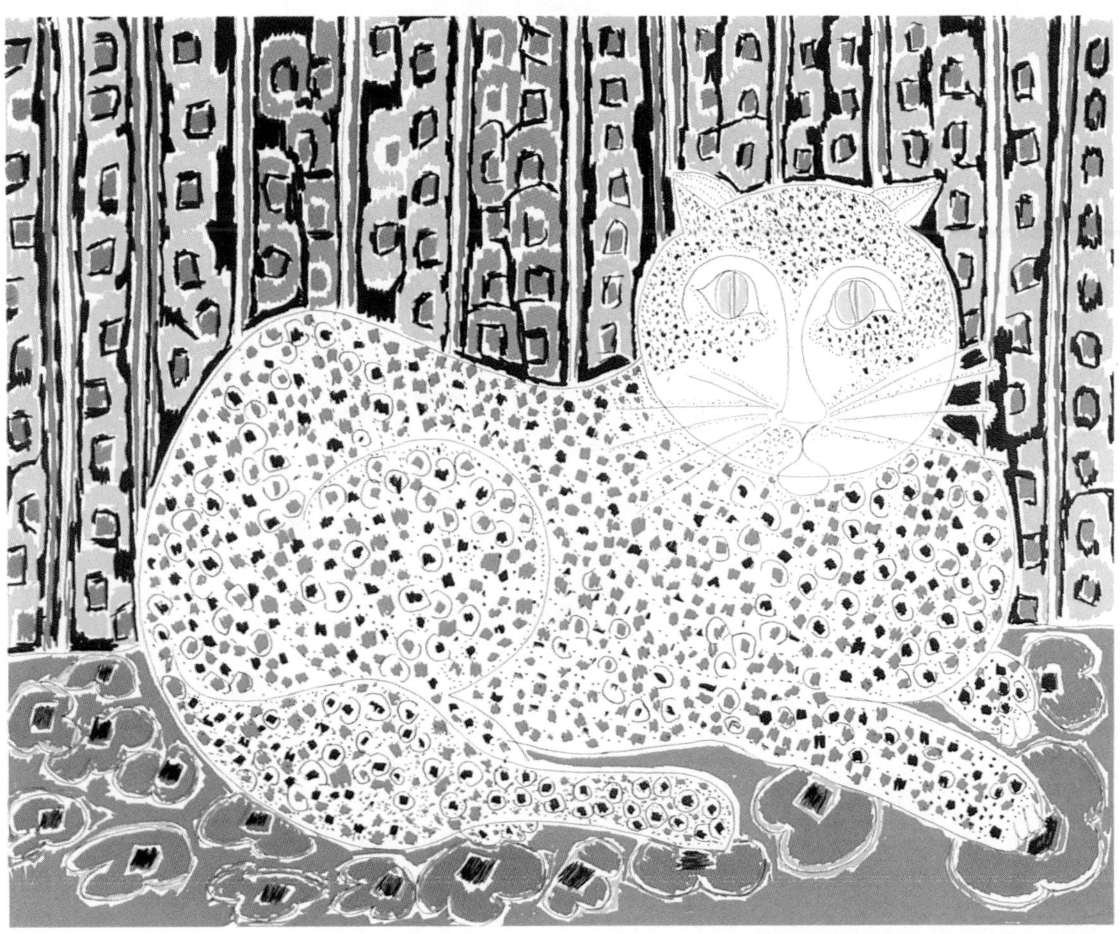

VANDERBILT CAT. An original color lithograph by Gloria Vanderbilt © 1974. An edition of 300, signed and numbered by the artist. 24"x32". 86-L

ONE-OF-A-KIND enameled copper boxes by Halcyon Days of England. These are hand painted to the customers' specifications, using photos. 1¾" diameter. 55-L

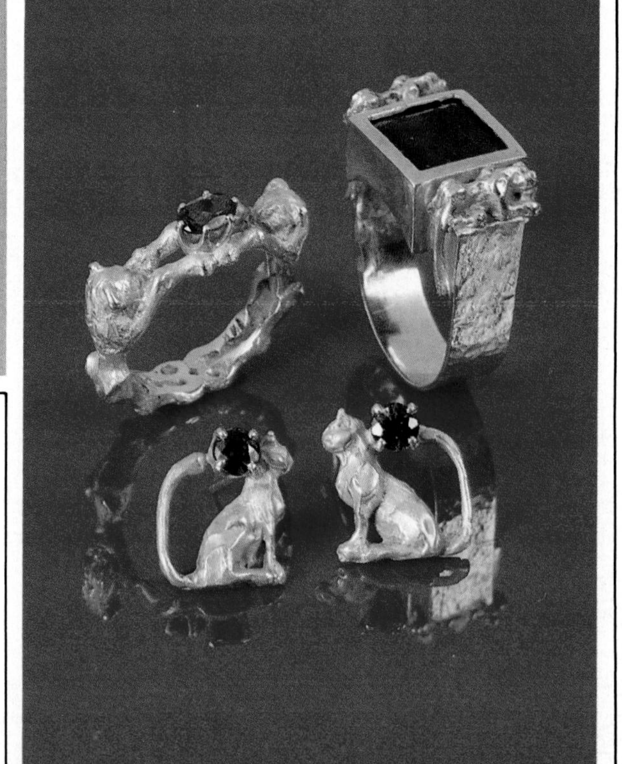

FABULOUS CATS designed by Linda Priest for Aaron Faber:

LION NECKLACE. 14K gold with diamond and carved malachite strung on onyx and malachite beads. Gold work is hand repousséd. 15-O

TWO-LIONS RING. The lions join to hold a green tourmaline. 15-M

LIONESSES RING, with a large lapis lazuli square. 15-N

CATS EARRINGS. 14K gold set with round sapphires. 15-M

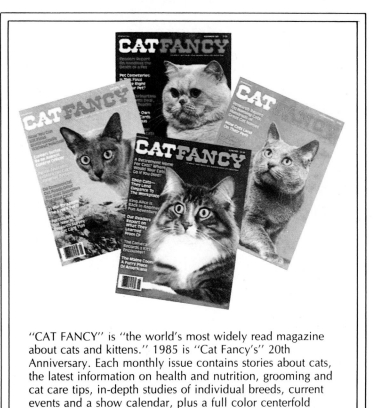

"CAT FANCY" is "the world's most widely read magazine about cats and kittens." 1985 is "Cat Fancy's" 20th Anniversary. Each monthly issue contains stories about cats, the latest information on health and nutrition, grooming and cat care tips, in-depth studies of individual breeds, current events and a show calendar, plus a full color centerfold poster. A subscription for 12 monthly issues, 85-B. You save on additional subscriptions.

CENTERFOLD POSTER from "Cat Fancy" magazine. Photograph is by Robert Pearcy, whose work appears regularly.

GARFIELD GUARDS this commodious ceramic cookie jar. It is three cookies high or 6"x9". (G866814) 8PS-C

"STILL LIFE WITH CAT" POSTER. Created from the original watercolor by Elizabeth Osborne. 36"x25¼" (1040) Unframed, 18-C; framed, 18-K

"BLACK & WHITE CAT" POSTER. Created from the original watercolor by Jacquie Marie Vaux, an American artist who specializes in animals, particularly cats. 34"x20". (1134) Unframed, 18-C; framed, 18-J

"MS. MUFFET" POSTER holds your attention. By Dick Ellescas. 26"x32". (822) Unframed, 18-C; framed, 18-K

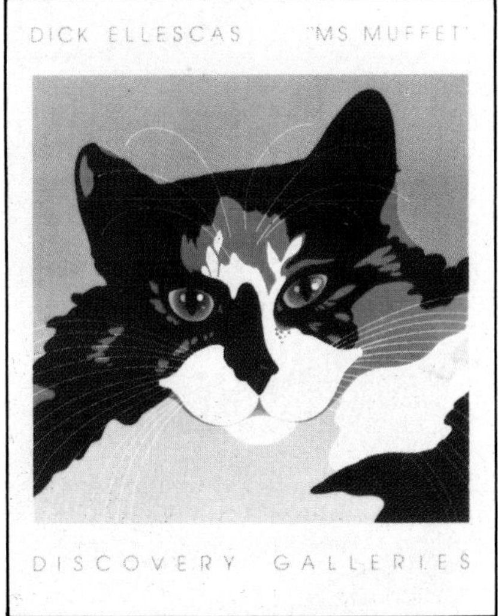

"CAT & CABOODLE" pet carrier. Soft-sided, over-the-shoulder bag with quilted nylon body intersected by sturdy nylon mesh. 14" top "comfort zipper" for petting on the move. Your cat enjoys a panoramic view, and proper ventilation. Secure and cozy. Washable. Can be stuffed under an airlines seat. 18"Lx9½"Wx11"H. Will carry up to a 25 lb. cat. 22-F

"CAT CATALOG." Experts from many fields have contributed to this book which contains more than 100 articles and 250 photographs and line illustrations exploring every aspect of the cat. 9"x11¼". Copyright © MCMLXXXVI by Workman Publishing Co., Inc. Used by permission of Arlington House, Inc. 93-A

SEND A FELINE to a friend. Six stand-up, die-cut cards by cat portraitist Susan Gray are perfect for any occasion. Package of six cards with envelopes. 2-A

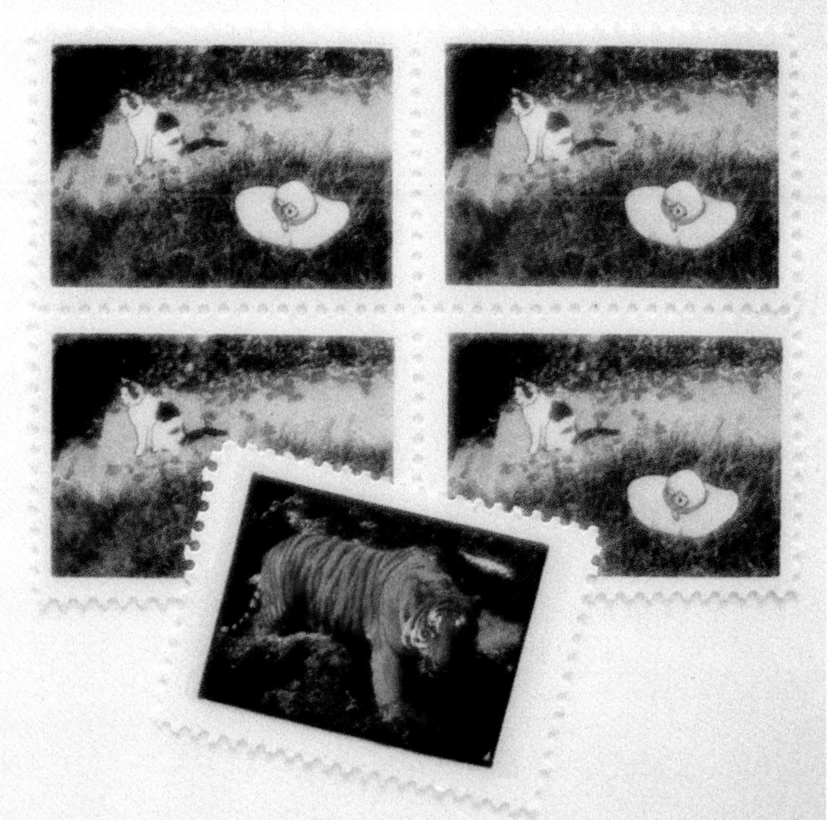

GENUINE POSTAGE STAMPS featuring cats are used to make these bookmarks, pins, earrings, keychains and magnets. Handmade, hand assembled and doubly laminated. See Source List for special offer, 39-A

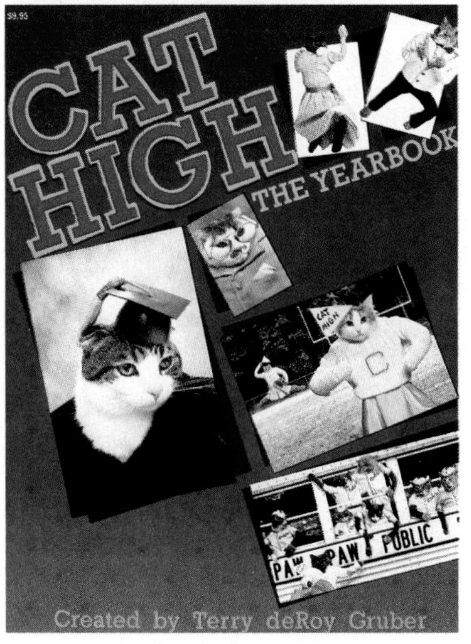


"GAMES YOU CAN PLAY WITH YOUR PUSSY CAT" by Ira Altman is a humorous paperback containing 96 pages of games to outwit, outmaneuver, outfox and outplay a clever cat. 71-A

"CAT HIGH" by Terry deRoy Gruber is a spoof on the typical high school yearbook. Cats in costume parody both teachers and students. Paperback. 49-A

REDWARE ORNAMENTS by Ned Foltz. May be hung or used as trivets. 16-B

"HOW TO PHOTOGRAPH CATS" by Robert Pearcy. With over 100,000 cat photographs to his credit, Pearcy explains some basics and the special tricks he uses to obtain his award-winning photographs. Illustrated. 56-B

YOUR CAT'S PHOTO ON STAMPS, gummed, perforated, ready for decorative use on correspondence, business cards and gifts. Any photo, 5"x7" or smaller, slide or Polaroid print (no negatives) can be made into a photo stamp. Your original is returned intact. © Sas Colby 1984. 100 stamps, 21-B

"CITY CATS COLLECTION." Made of dishwasher safe white porcelain. Black and white Tom Cat and Calico Cat families appear on a red brick background. The matching accessories include plates, jar with spoon, mugs and tea mug sets, spoon rests, salt and pepper shakers, and a ½ lb. cat tin made in England. 102A through 102D

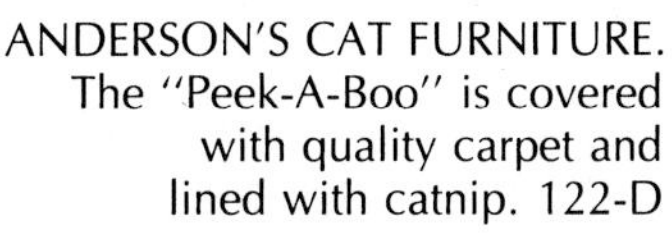

ANDERSON'S CAT FURNITURE. The "Peek-A-Boo" is covered with quality carpet and lined with catnip. 122-D

"COUNTRY CAT COLLECTION": Four kinds of cats and kittens handpainted on ceramic. A complete line of matching decorative and functional accessories, including light switch wall plates, spoonrests, hooks, picture frames, mugs, ceramic planters, figurines, porcelain bisque musicals, and more. 102A through 102D

"THE OWL AND THE PUSSYCAT." Edward Lear's nonsense classic is reinterpreted here by illustrator Hilary Knight, the illustrator of "Eloise at the Plaza" and many other books for children. 97-B

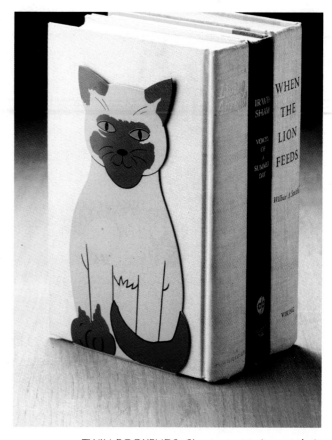

TWIN BOOKENDS. Siamese cat twins put their backs flat to the books. Hand painted enameled metal. Each 7¼"x3¾". (G569475) Pr., 8HH-A

BOOKMARKS/PINKEEPERS. Set of three colorful felt kittens. 2"x12". (8441) 57-A

"MILLIONS OF CATS." This classic American picture book by Wanda Gag tells the tale of a gentle peasant who goes off in search of one kitten, and returns home with millions of cats. Hardcover, 72-A. Paper, 72-A

MILLIONS OF CATS

BY WANDA GÁG

NIGHT LIGHT. Soft light filters through amber glass with inquisitive cat perched on the edge. Metal base with on/off switch. Includes bulb. 5" high. (8405; 57-B

CAT SHAPED CHRISTMAS STOCKING with large pouch to fill with goodies for kitty. Red, green, 75-A

19TH CENTURY folk art designs are reproduced in these hand screened cats. They are available in both kit form or already sewn and stuffed. "Tabby Cat." 14" high. Stuffed, 52-B. Kit, 52-A. "Green-eyed Kittens." 6" high. Stuffed, 52-A. Kit, 52-A. "Tabby Kittens" also available. 52-A

RED HEART SHAPED CHRISTMAS ORNAMENTS, personalized with your cat's name and "Christmas 1985." With personalization, 75-A

PET CHRISTMAS STOCKING of felt with crocheted trim and bells. Can be personalized, in a variety of red, green and white combinations. Each, 75-A; small extra charge for personalizing.

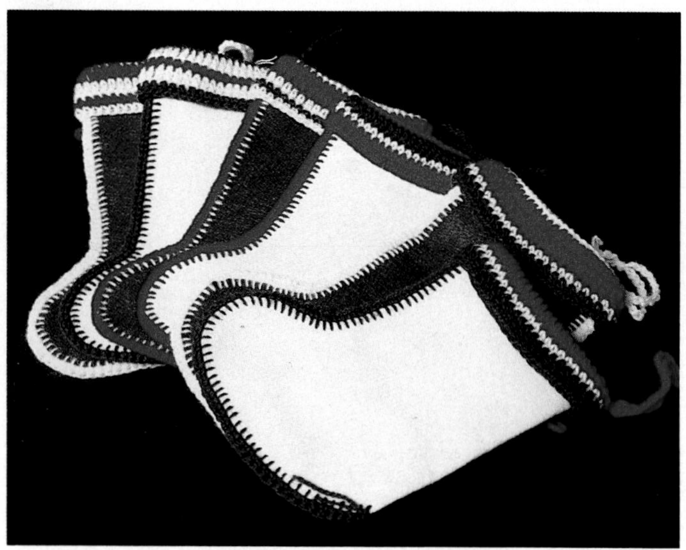

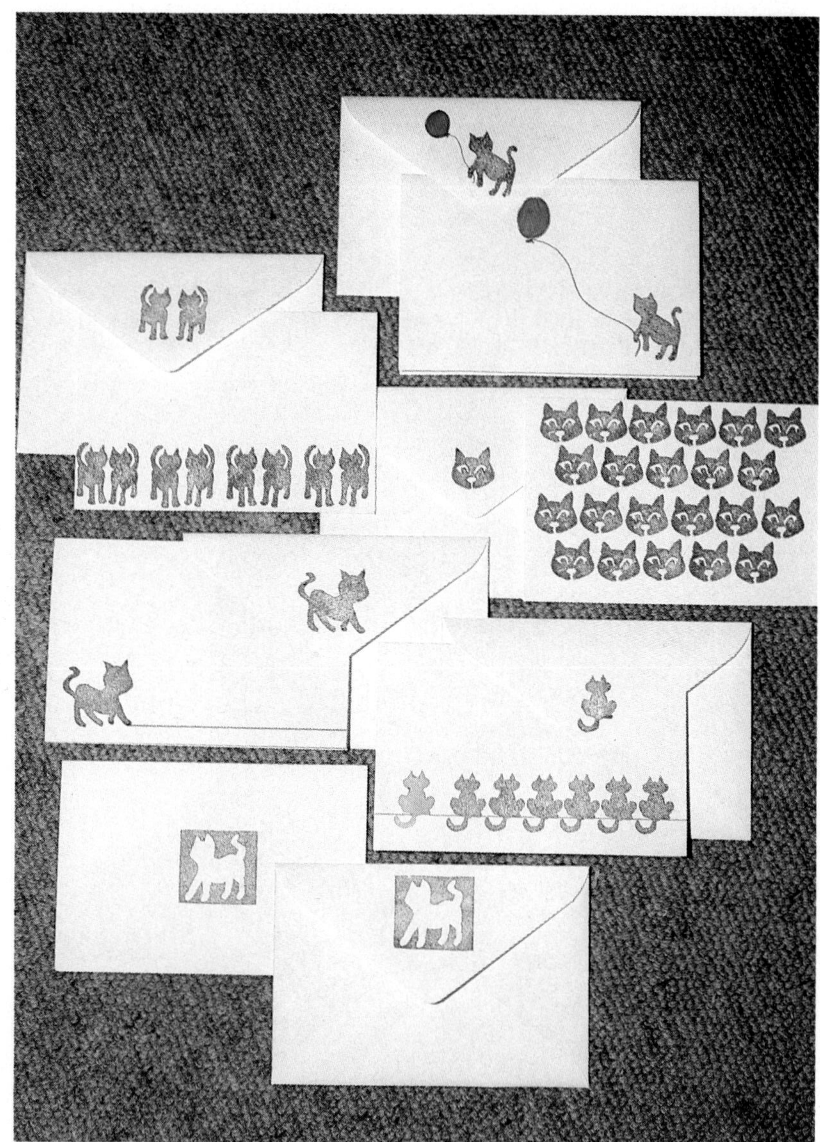

RUBBER STAMP ART. Notecards and envelopes feature six different cat motifs. Hand stamped. 4"x6". Sets of 6 or 12. 28-A

PERSIAN CAT BLOUSE. Hand painted, sparked with rhinestones at the eyes. In polyester. One size fits up to 16. Black. (J770317A) 8HA-F

THREE GLITTERING CATS decorate these fleecy sweatshirts. Ribbed cuffs on long sleeves and bottom. Washable acrylic knit. White or black. S (6-8), M (10-12), L (14). (J272484) 8CC-B

BEADED BAG. Evening bag with shoulder strap features glittering cat face. 55-D

SILK KOMONO. All handmade, with etching applied to silk. Signed and numbered by artist Bethia Brehmer. 70-L

ANTIQUE PIN. Three 18k gold kittens, each with a 2 pt. round diamond in its collar. From base, three fine white round diamonds (total wgt. of diamonds 60 pts.) Circa 1910. © 1984 Aaron Faber Gallery. 15-O

CAT FANS. Silk-screened and hand painted by American artisan Cynthia Winika. 55-B

STONEWARE BOWLS. Tiny hearts and your cat's name are repeated around the rim of a high-fired stoneware bowl. Lettering is impressed into the clay. Approx. 7″ diameter and 2″ high. Choice of cobalt blue, brick, speckled tan and speckled white. 87-C

PAPER DOLLS. A "Victorian Cat Family" by Evelyn Gathings has clothing, furniture, toys, and more—all in full color. 95-A

"THE BOOK OF THE CAT." Everything you ever wanted to know about cats, from evolution to health care to breeding and showing; hundreds of photographs and drawings. Paperback. 8½″x11¼″. 61-B

LYNN HOLLYN'S "TOWN AND COUNTRY CAT" has softly-toned paintings by Robert Goldstrom. *Publishers Weekly* called this book "a must for cat lovers." © 1982 Lynn Hollyn 3-B; "TOWN AND COUNTRY POSTCARD PORTFOLIO." The packet contains six 5″x7″ postcards that feature reproductions from Lynn Hollyn's whimsical book "Town and Country Cat." © 1982 Lynn Hollyn 3-A

"THE KITTY-CAT COOKBOOK" by Barbara Ellen Benson is an illustrated book of recipes for cats to enjoy on holidays and special occasions. It also includes ideas for wholesome change-of-pace foods for your cat. Recipes include Catnip Cobbler, Mackerel Mousse and Salmon Supreme. 35-A

YOUR CAT'S PORTRAIT in oil on wood by animal portraitist Susan Gray. Portraits are appxoimately 12″x15″ unframed. 2-N

"THE CAT'S PAJAMAS" in Houston, is both a deluxe boarding and grooming facility for cats (and only cats); and a place to buy a great variety of items for cats and cat lovers. Some of these items are shown on this page, others elsewhere in the book.

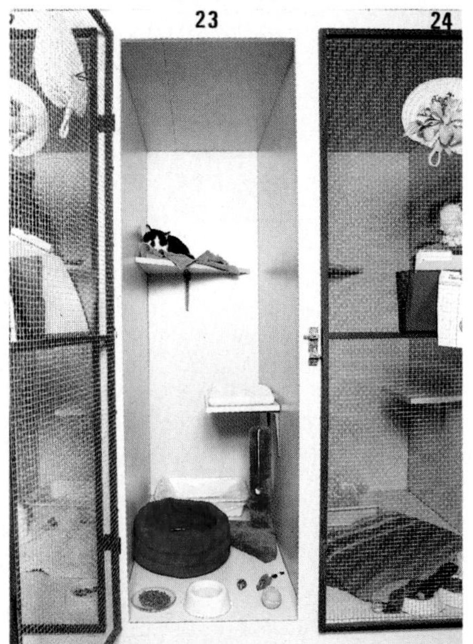

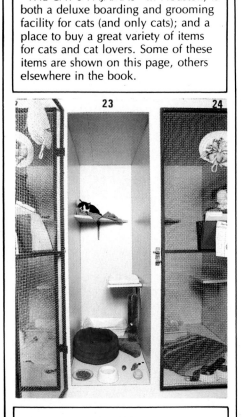

OVERSIZE SUITES filled with the cat's favorite things, and offering lofty climbing and sleeping ledges, pamper the temporary boarder.

CAT SWEATERS, hand crocheted by Aunt Velma to keep cats warm in winter. Assorted designer colors. You can send for a sizing chart and color choices. 75-B

MINI TOTE BAGS are 6"x6", and have handles. Could be a child's first handbag. Blue with white or red with yellow. Each, 75-A

ANDERSON'S CAT FUNITURE. The "Hideaway" is covered with top quality carpet and lined with fresh catnip. 75-E

PET HAIR PICKUPS remove pet hair and lint from clothes and furniture. Just peel off the used piece of tape and start fresh. 75-A. Refills available.

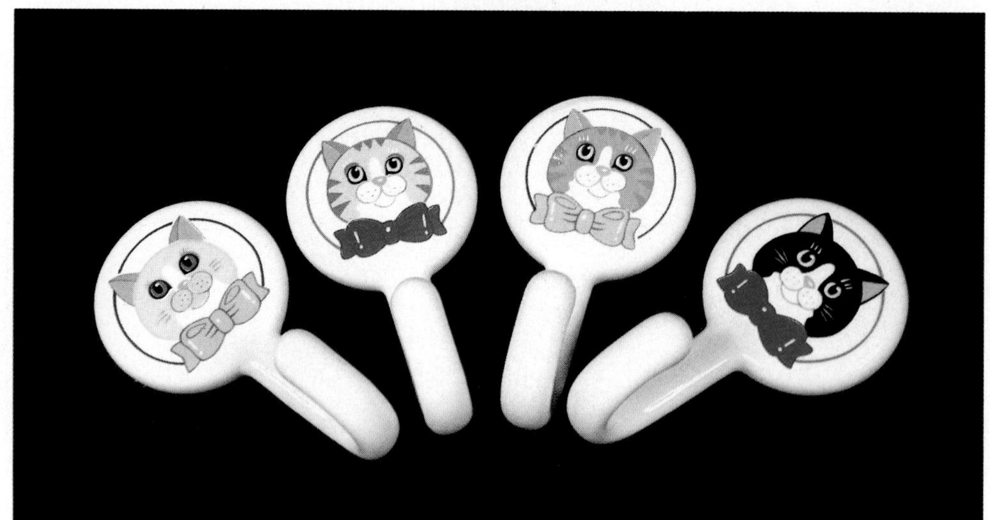

CATFACE HOOKS. Self adhesive. Black, orange, tan or gray faces. Each, 75-A; set of four, assorted, 75-B

A PORTRAIT OF YOUR CAT. Artist Peter Nichols will capture your cat's likeness and personality in full color pastel or oils. He works from the photo(s) you send him. Pastel 11″x14″, approx. 14″x18″ matted. 103-I; Oil on canvas, ready to frame, 14″x18″. 103-K

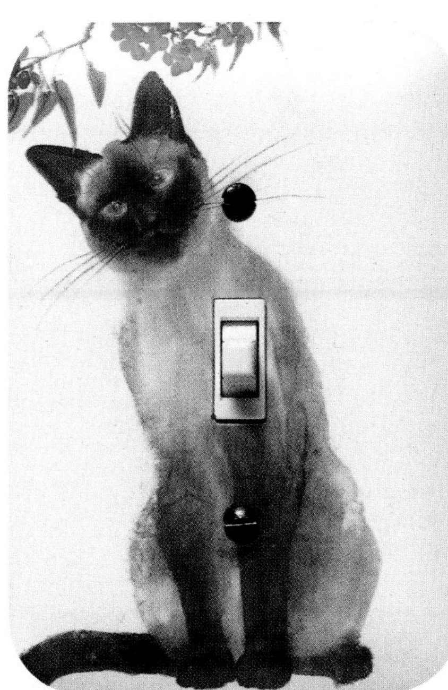

SWITCH PLATE with laminated silkscreen print. Metal, with mounting screws. 3½″x5″. (79213) 58PP-A

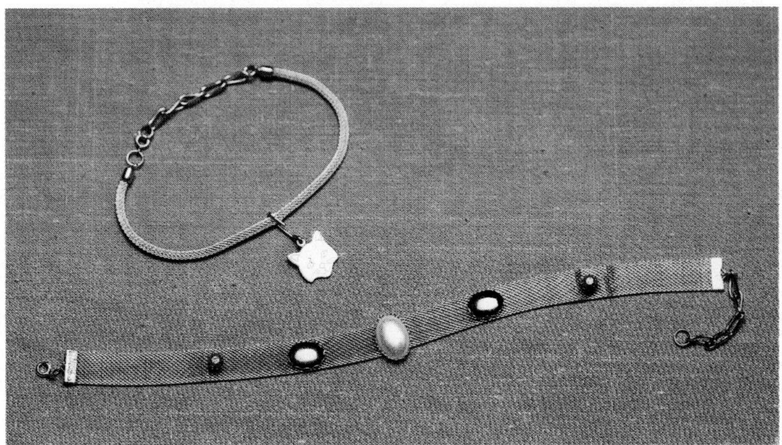

JEWELRY FOR A FELINE is useful as well as ornamental. The jeweled cat collar and I.D. tag are unique identification, helpful if the cat should get lost. Collar (J573972) 8HH-A; I.D. Tag (specify name) (J573980P) 8HH-A

ORNAMENTS for Christmas tree or wreath, nursery wall or shade pulls; a party favor too. Hand crafted, hand painted both sides. Wood and other natural materials. 3″x4″. (16023) 58PP-B

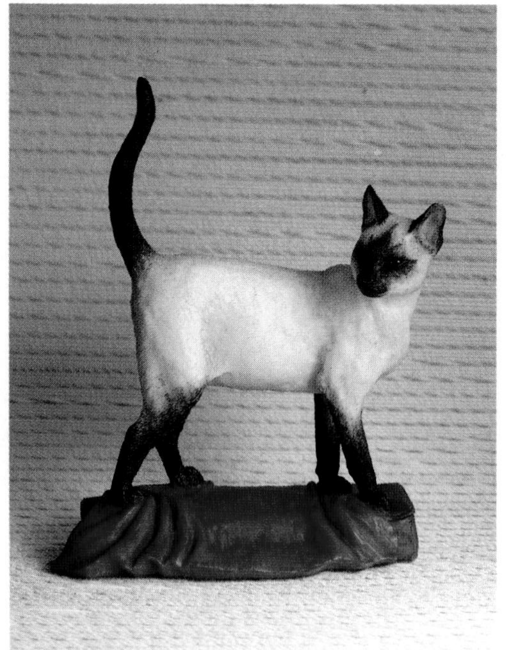

SEALPOINT SIAMESE. Detailed portrayal hand crafted in Scotland of cold cast porcelain. 3½″ x4½″. (54993) 58PP-E

"FINGERTALES" is a take-along toy for trips. It lets you stage a one-act play on the palm of your hand. 23-B

NOTE CARDS. Set of six 5″x7″ cards with envelopes. (M110) 40-A

"COUNTRY CAT COLLECTION." A complete line of functional and decorative accessories of hand painted ceramic. 102-A through 102-D

"PURRRRR! The Newsletter for Cat Lovers" is available by subscription. If you send it as a gift, *Purrrrr!* will include a gift card with the first copy. Issues contain practical articles on pets, products, medical news. Book reviews, etc. and humor too. Six issues, 107-A; twelve issues, 107-B

"IN THE COMPANY OF CATS." This annual calendar benefits The Humane Society of the United States. Full-color photos with quotations and lots of writing room. 12"x12". (M928) 40-A

TERRA COTTA CATS. Handpainted ceramic cats are combined with terra cotta for matching kitchen accessories. There are terra cotta jars, napkin holders, jam jars with spoon, covered boxes, ceramic salt and pepper shakers, tea pots and pitchers, flower vases, mugs of various design, cat dishes, and a cat and shoe toothpick holder. From 102A through 102D

HOOKED RUGS for floor or wall. 100% wool, from China. "Oriental Prince" (single cat) 24"Wx35"L. (180) 24-K; "Feline Frolics" 28"Wx39½". (181) 24-K. Part of the Cat Companion Collection™

"CATLAP." Triple layers of quilted cotton and heavy denim protect knits and other fabrics (as well as your skin) from your cat's claws. One size (22"x15") fits all laps. Red calico with blue or green trim, or blue calico with red trim. 106-B

"CATCH THE MOUSIE" toy. The Mousie is 100% sheepskin and leather in tan, black, gray, or white. Includes stick for exciting Mousie action. 99-A

MILTON GLASER POSTER for The Animal Relief Fund of the Hamptons. Title: "Creatures Large and Small." 24"x36" in offset lithography. © Milton Glaser. 36-B

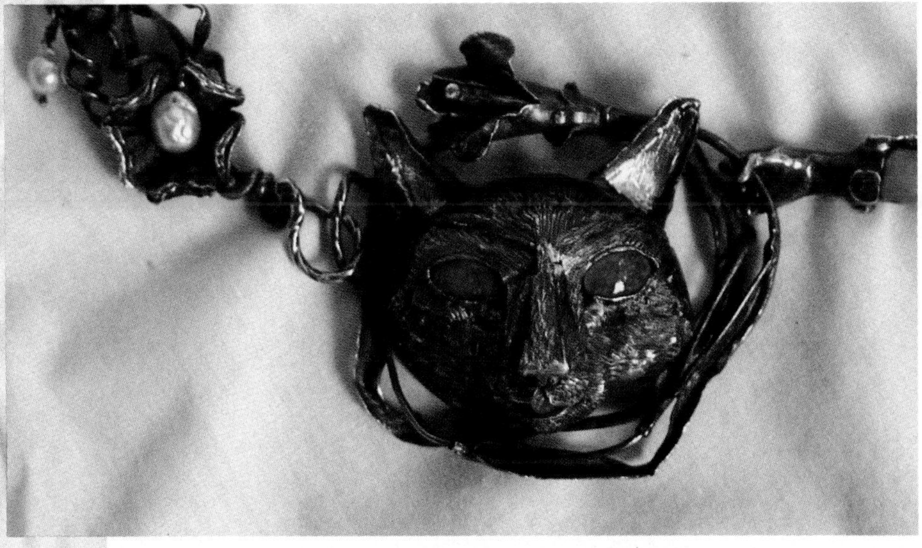

ONE-OF-A-KIND combination necklace, belt, or brooch. This "medieval" sculpture is by Torben Hardenberg, "one of Denmark's most imaginative jewelry designers." It is made to order of silver, coral, pearls, and turquoise, and has sapphire eyes. 108-P

GROOMING AIDS. Porcelain miniatures, hand crafted and hand painted. Gift boxed. Cache for small items, earrings, 8x3¾x5″ (G920652) 8-B; Caddy for makeup tools, 6x2¾x3½″ (G920678) 8-A; Lint Brush has fabric bottom. 6x2¾x3½″ (G920660) 8-A; Nail Brush with nylon bristles. Approx. 3x2x3″ (G920686) 8AY-A

"CAT NAMES" by Eleanora Walker with illustrations by Alan Daniel. Over 4000 names, and some ideas on how to find the perfect one for your cat. Paperback. 56-A

CAT WITH YARN. Bisque porcelain music box plays "Memories." 5x3x3½" high. (J869214) 8PS-C

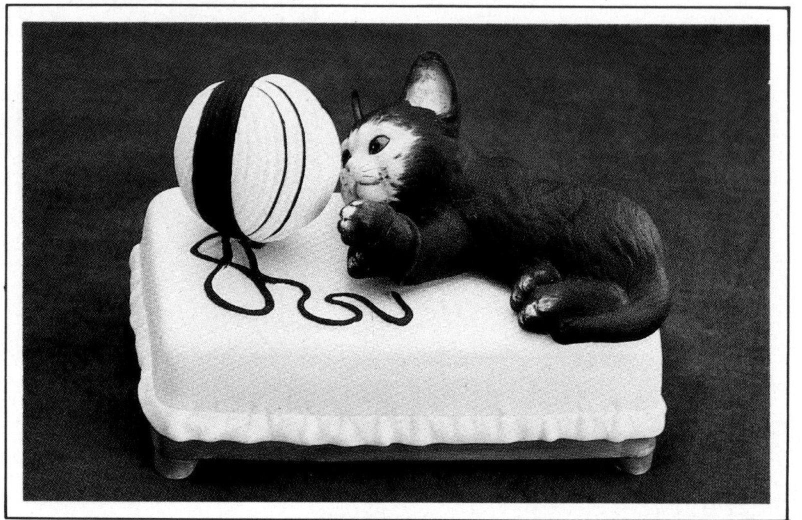

KITTY CAT HOLIDAY WRAPS. Bags and sturdy fiberboard boxes are reusable gift wraps that require no cutting or taping. 2 large boxes (9x5x7"); 3 small boxes (3⅞x3⅞x7"); 4 small bags and tags (8¼x4¼x12¾"); 3 large bags and tags (6x3x10¾"). Enough to wrap 12 gifts. (J869248) 8PS-A

SANDRA BOYNTON'S whimsical cats adorn wallpaper, wall borders and fabric. "The Feline is Mutual" border: per yd., 90-A. "Cat in the Moon" fabric: per yd., 90-C. "Cat in the Moon" wallpaper: per roll, 90-C

STENCILED CAT on muslin with ruffle, to hang on the wall. On 8″ hoop. 33-B

"KITTENS" is the first of a series of Signature Prints, signed, limited editions, offered by Robert Pearcy, The Animal Photographer. His photography appears frequently on the covers and within *Cat Fancy* magazine and other well known specialized animal publications; and on calendars, greeting cards and posters. "Kittens," 11″x14″, ready for framing. 51-C

LARGE STENCILED CAT is 15″ high and beribboned. Set it in your entry hall to greet your guests. 33-A

SALT AND PEPPER SHAKERS.
Hand painted bone china.
(G673988) 2 pc. set, 8NH-A

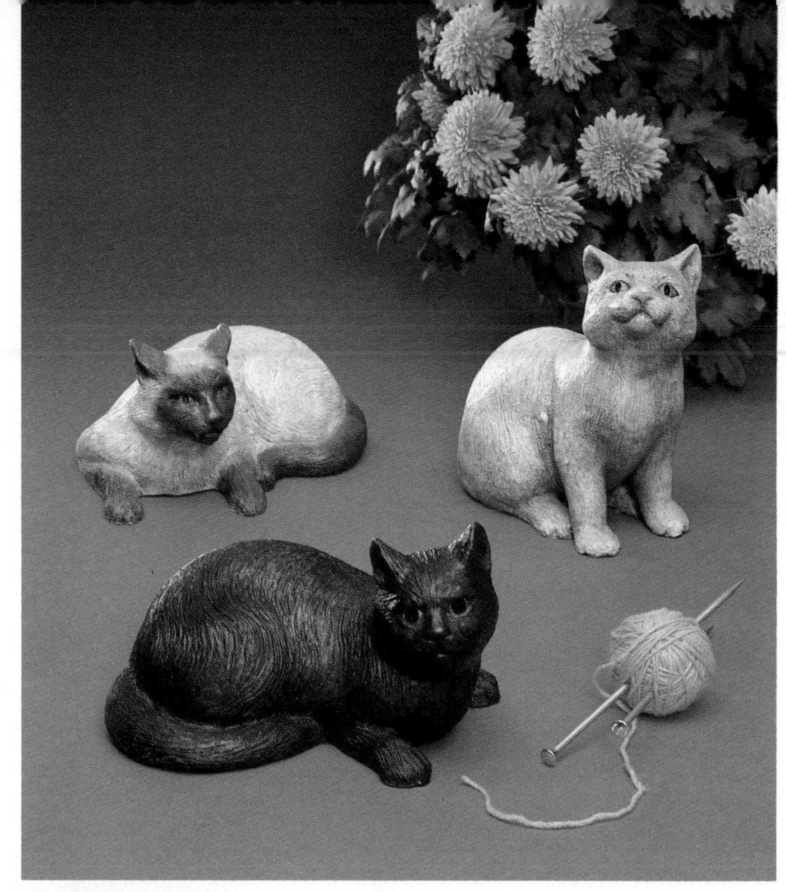

TINKER, GINSENG AND SCHEHERAZADE are one-of-a-kind originals in terra cotta and glaze. Signed by the artist, Ann Fisher. Each is also available in a Limited Edition, slightly smaller, of hand painted ceramic, cast from the original. Each, 24-L. Limited Edition, 24-K. Part of The Cat Companion Collection™.

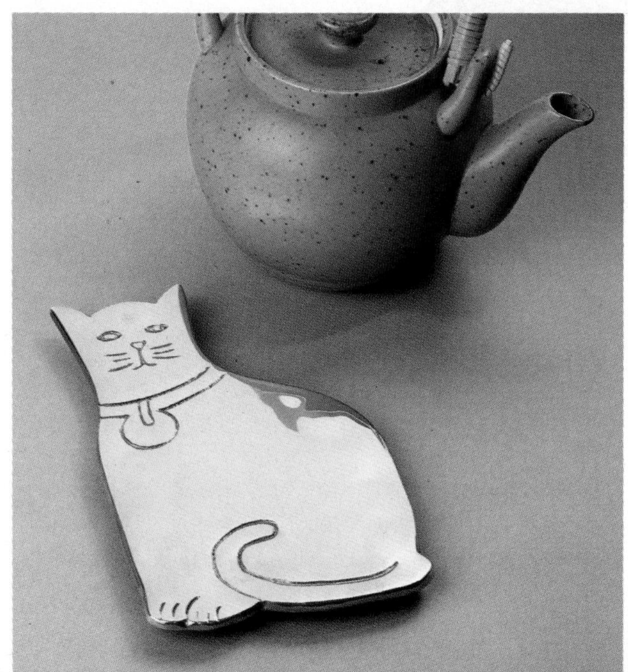

SOLID BRASS TRIVET. Practical table accessory looks good on counter or shelf as well. Rubber footed underside prevents scratches. 7½"H (G678888) 8NH-A

LIFE-LIKE ANGORA cat of genuine icelandic lamb fur. Emerald green eyes, pink felt ears and nose. Silky satin pink bows. Hand embroidered details. 2′3″ long. (5450411) 8OV-A

"BABY FACE" is one of artist Patricia McLaughlin's original scratchboard Limited Edition prints, signed and numbered. This design, and many others, are also available on notecards, birthday cards, postcards, etc. Black and White print, 5″x7″ unmatted, 38-B; other items, mostly 38-A

CROSS STITCH CHRISTMAS ORNAMENTS. Assorted designs. 75-A

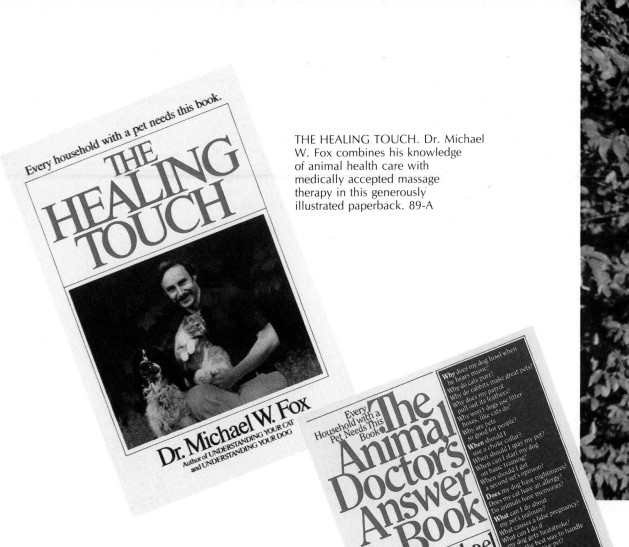

THE HEALING TOUCH. Dr. Michael W. Fox combines his knowledge of animal health care with medically accepted massage therapy in this generously illustrated paperback. 89-A

PET CARRIER. This washable corduroy carrier is for the cat who likes the security of being close to you. S for cats up to 5 lbs.; M to 10 lbs.; L to 18 lbs. 37-C

Every Household with a Pet Needs This Book.
The Animal Doctor's Answer Book
Dr. Michael W. Fox
Director, Institute of Animal Problems of the Humane Society of the United States
Author of *Understanding Your Dog* and *Understanding Your Cat*

America's most respected and popular veterinarian and animal psychologist answers more than 1,000 questions about the care and behavior of cats, dogs, fish, birds, rabbits, hamsters, and other companion animals

**Why** does my dog howl when he hears music?
Why do cats purr?
Why do rabbits make great pets?
Why does my parrot pull out its feathers?
Why won't dogs use litter boxes, like cats do?
Why are pets so good for people?
**When** should I use a choke collar?
When should I spay my pet?
When can I start my dog on basic training?
When should I get a second vet's opinion?
**Does** my dog have nightmares?
Does my cat have an allergy?
Do animals have memories?
**What** can I do about my pet's jealousy?
What causes a false pregnancy?
What can I do if my dog gets heatstroke?
What's the best way to handle my hyperactive pet?
What are the facts about feline leukemia?
What can I do about my dog's bad breath?
What breed of cat might be safe for people with allergies?
**How** can I survive the first nights with my new puppy?
How can I tell when my animal is in pain?
How can I keep my bird from going stir-crazy?
How can I tell if my hamster is expecting?
How often should my pet see a vet for vaccinations and exams?
How can I keep my pet from being lonely when I'm not there?
How many times a year can my cat get pregnant?

THE ANIMAL DOCTOR'S ANSWER BOOK by Dr. Michael W. Fox. A compendium of expert knowledge and animal lore that answers 1000 questions about the care and behavior of cats and other companion animals. Hardcover or paperback. 89-B

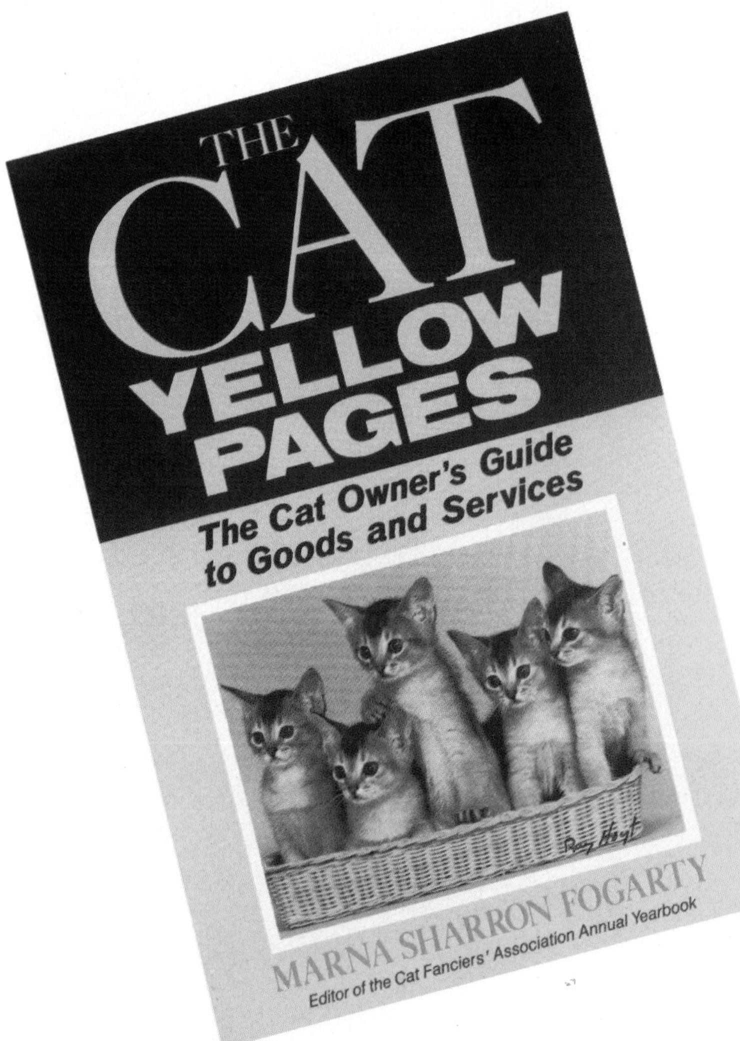


FISH SHAPED CARPET TOY filled with fresh catnip. Long, soft pull cord attached. Tan, rose, green. 75-A

"THE CAT YELLOW PAGES. The Cat Owner's Guide to Goods and Services." Extensive listing includes care tips, hotlines, humane societies. By Marna Sharron Fogarty, Dir. of Publications for The Cat Fancier's Association. 60 black & white photos, 224 pages, 6"x9". 65-B

CRITTER CORALE. This dome-like structure makes a comfortable sleeping niche with its soft, furry pad. Completely washable. 12"x16"x13" (H717918) ROG80-A

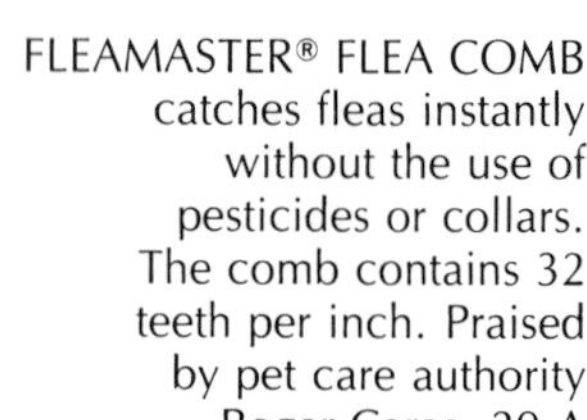

FLEAMASTER® FLEA COMB catches fleas instantly without the use of pesticides or collars. The comb contains 32 teeth per inch. Praised by pet care authority Roger Caras. 20-A

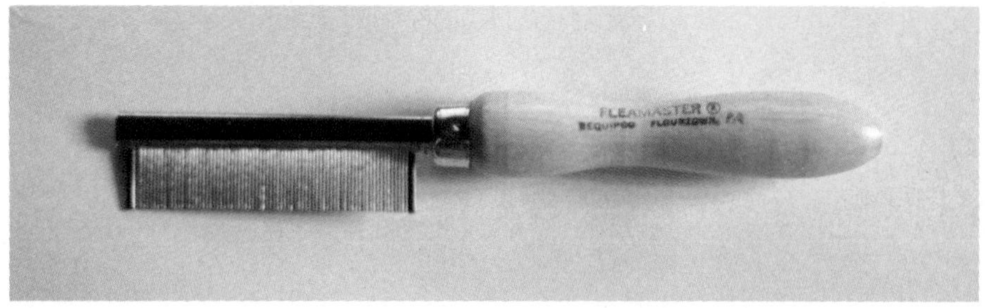

"PUSS IN BOOTS" boot stuffers keep boots tidy and pleasantly scented. Can also stand alone, upright, to freshen closet. 22"H. Yellow, green, red, blue or purple. Each, 102-B

SOFT STUFFED TOYS by Avanti: Siamese mama and kittens, velcro attached. 20". 102-C; Sitting Himalayan with ice blue eyes. 10". 102-C

"KITTY KATFISH" collection: Towel, apron, potholder and mitt. Matching mugs available. 102-A through 102-B

HAND CRAFTED PILLOWS AND SACHETS, including a baby pillow (in 2 sizes) decorated with Baby Breath, satin ribbon and a little bell. As shown, or see swatches. 102-A through 102-C

LONG-HAIRED FEMALE CALICO is a soft stuffed toy by Avanti. 14″. 102-F

CHILDREN'S SAFETY SCISSORS have rounded edges. Comes with its own tag for child's name, and a protective sleeve. 102-A

LARGE SEATED CAT. The original bronze statuette dates from the 26th Dynasty (663-525 B.C.). Reproduced in cold cast bronze with small gold-plated earrings. Height including base, 7″. 44-D

EGYPTIAN CAT PENDANT. On 16″ gold-plated chain. 44-B

EGYPTIAN CAT EARRINGS are for pierced ears only. Gold-plated metal. 44-B

SMALL SACRED CAT. The original is from the late-period (7th to 1st centuries B.C.). Gold-plated metal. 1¾″ in height. 44-B

THE INDISPENSABLE CAT by J.C. Suares. This exquisite book documents the cat's relationship to people in history, literature, and art. Includes the works of great artists and writers from Manet to Mark Twain. Cloth, 192 pages. 44-C

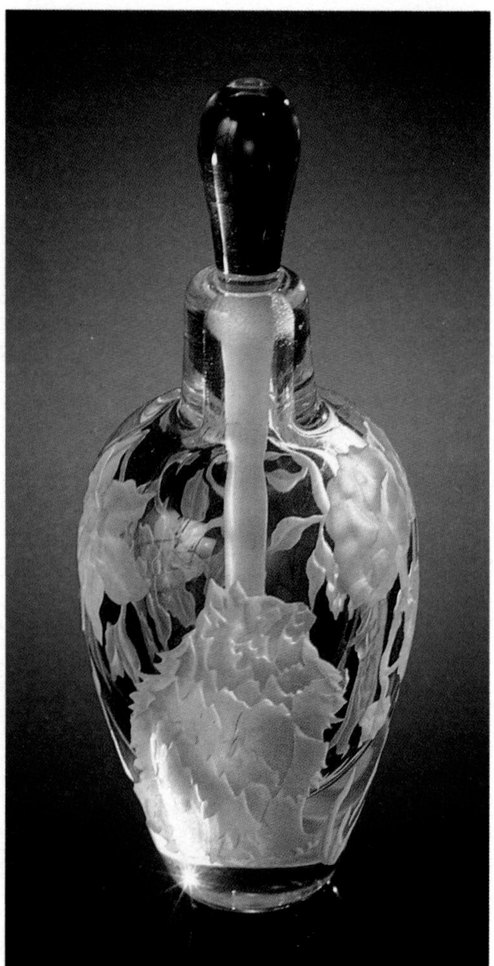

PERFUME FLACON. Hand etched perfume bottle by Phyllis Nourot. Each piece is signed and registered. 1 fl. oz. size, 4⅝"x1¾". (140) 24-L

CATS TELEPHONE/ADDRESS BOOK. Adapted from a hand colored lithograph by Theophile A. Steinlen (French, 1859-1923). 5"x8". 44-B

CATS MEMO BOX. With same image as above, the box holds 200 blank standard-size leaves. 4½"x6¼". 44-B

# 78

PENDANTS, EARRINGS, PINS AND CHAINS in solid 14k gold with diamonds and other gems: Reaching Cat; Largest "Tummy" Cat pendant; Trio of Cats, 16" or 18" chain; "Sandy" Kitten; Reaching Longhair Kitten; Sapphire or Topaz Eye Cat; Cat on a Shelf reaching for his toy, a 12pt. diamond; "Persian" bracelet; Opal Whimsey Cat earrings; "Lorena" style earrings. Prices range from 31-D to 31-M.

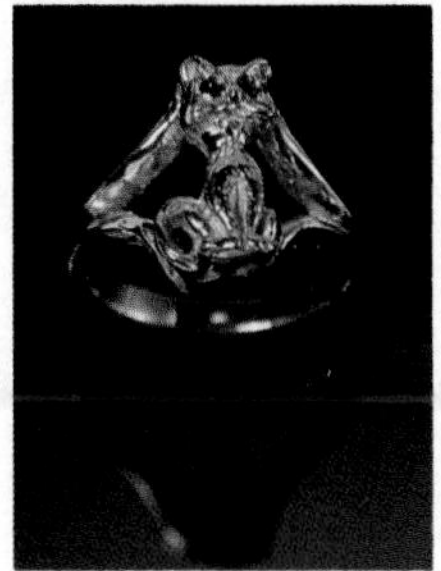

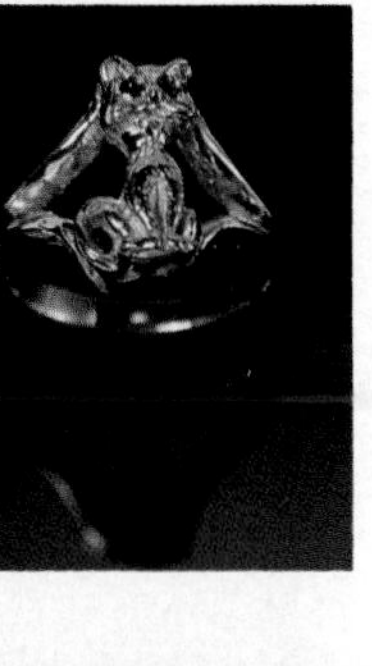

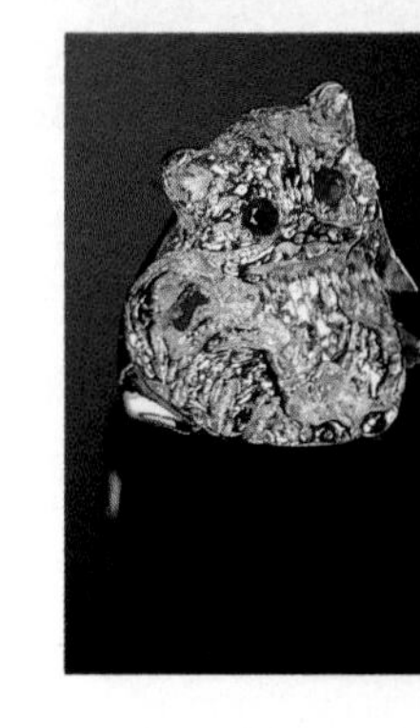

CAT MOTIF RINGS of solid 14k gold, with gem eyes: Large "Tummy" Cat; Lamplighter Cat; "Karen" style cat; Sapphire Eye Cat; Kitten with gem "Ball" and eyes to match; "Sweet Fluffin"; "Archie" the arch cat ring. Prices range from 31-I to 31-L.

VIENNA BRONZE CAT. Hand crafted and hand painted. 2⅛″ long. (F627PO) 88-K

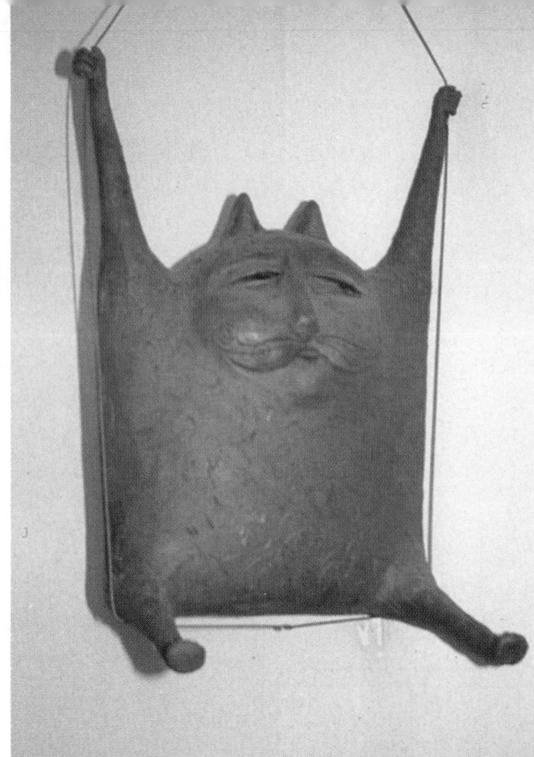

HANGING CAT by ceramic sculptor/potter Al Davis. 28″x16″. 70-L

MEXICAN CATS. Hand painted pottery with nature motifs. 8″x4″. 70-A

FAT CAT by ceramic sculptor/potter Al Davis has bright red tongue. 29″x18″. 70-L

"SHERRICATS" are small, perky, finely detailed ceramic figurines, individually signed. Just the right size for the odd little corner, view box, or tiny shelf.

MAGNETS, showing the ten colors available. The center one is the "Sherricats" logo. Each, 29-A

"PADDY PAWS" SERIES: Larger "Sherricats," more actively positioned and done with a touch of humor. They range from 2½"H (standing) to 3½"L, and come in a variety of poses, breeds and colors. Just a few are shown here. Each, 29-A

GANG of small cats. Ceramic miniatures by "Sherricats." 29-A

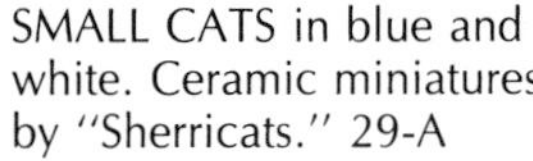

SMALL CATS in blue and white. Ceramic miniatures by "Sherricats." 29-A

MORE "PADDY PAWS" described on facing page.

FAMILY OF BLACK CATS ranging in size from 2½"H to 1¼"L. 29-A

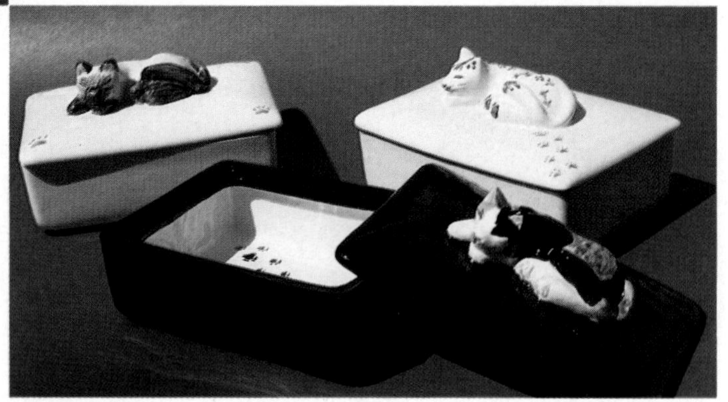

SLEEPING CAT BOX. Sleeper left his paw print inside the box before he went to sleep. 3½" high. 29-B; LARGE BOX, showing three styles of paw print. 5½"Lx4"Wx3"H. 29-B. Assorted colors.

"TALE OF A CAT" © MONEY CLIP in Sterling Silver (135) 24-K; or in 14K gold (136) 24-L; and can be ordered with emerald eyes. (One hundred dollar bill NOT included.) Part of The Cat Companion Collection™.

"WHAT TO NAME THE CAT" by Thelma Kandel with drawings by Mimi Vang Olsen. Thousands of cat names drawn from a variety of sources, from old standbys to the truly exotic. Paperback. 61-A

"THE CAT WHO WENT TO HEAVEN" by Elizabeth Coatsworth has illustrations by Lynd Ward. This story of a cat and a poor Japanese artist won the Newbery Medal. 97-A

"THE NEEDLEPOINT CAT" by William Halsey Brister. Twenty-four needlepoint projects with cat subjects include wall hangings, eyeglass cases, doorstops, and even suspenders. Complete step-by-step instructions. Hardcover. 80-B

MARCOLIN CRYSTAL CAT is hand sculptured, over 24% lead crystal, and has an overall height of about 10". (B-095) 82-G

SCRIMSHAW PENDANTS AND EARRINGS by Mimi Ide Suverkrup. "Puss and Boots" pendant (137) 24-D; "Siamese" pendant (138) 24-B; "Kitten" earrings for pierced ears (139) 24-C. Pendant chains not included; can be ordered separately. Part of The Cat Companion Collection™.

FIRESCREENS signed by the artist, Florence Bird. Hand crafted, with steel frames. Heavy gauge mesh screen and multiple panels are copper hinged. "Running Free"—The big cats of the Serengeti. Center panel 30"Hx40"W. Side panels each 30"Hx12½"W (177). On facing page, "Moon Cat". Center panel 37"Hx24"W. Side panels each 29½"Hx12"W. "Kitten Fancy". 30"Hx39¾"W at base. (179) Each screen, 24-L. Part of The Cat Companion Collection™.

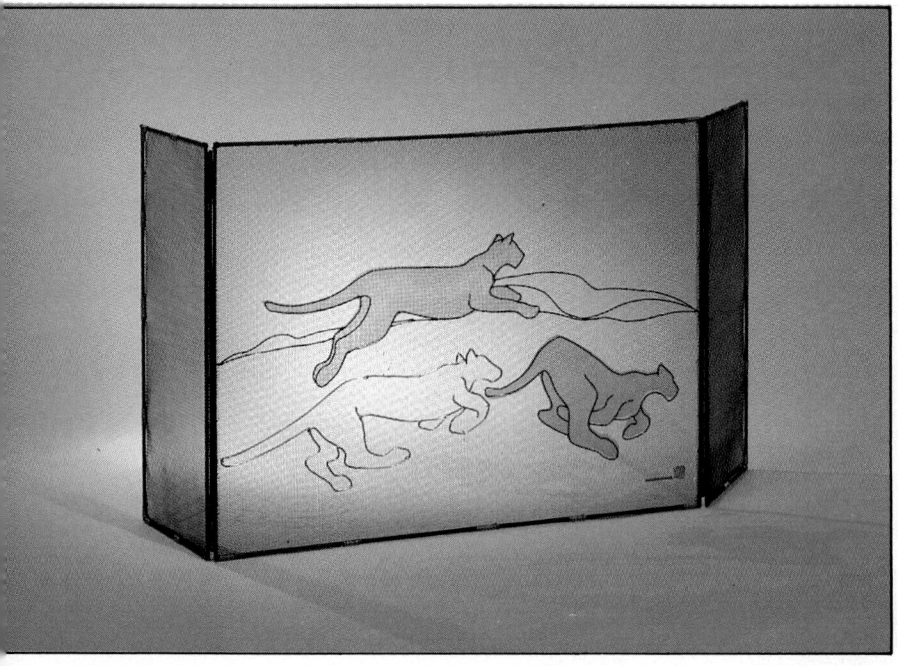

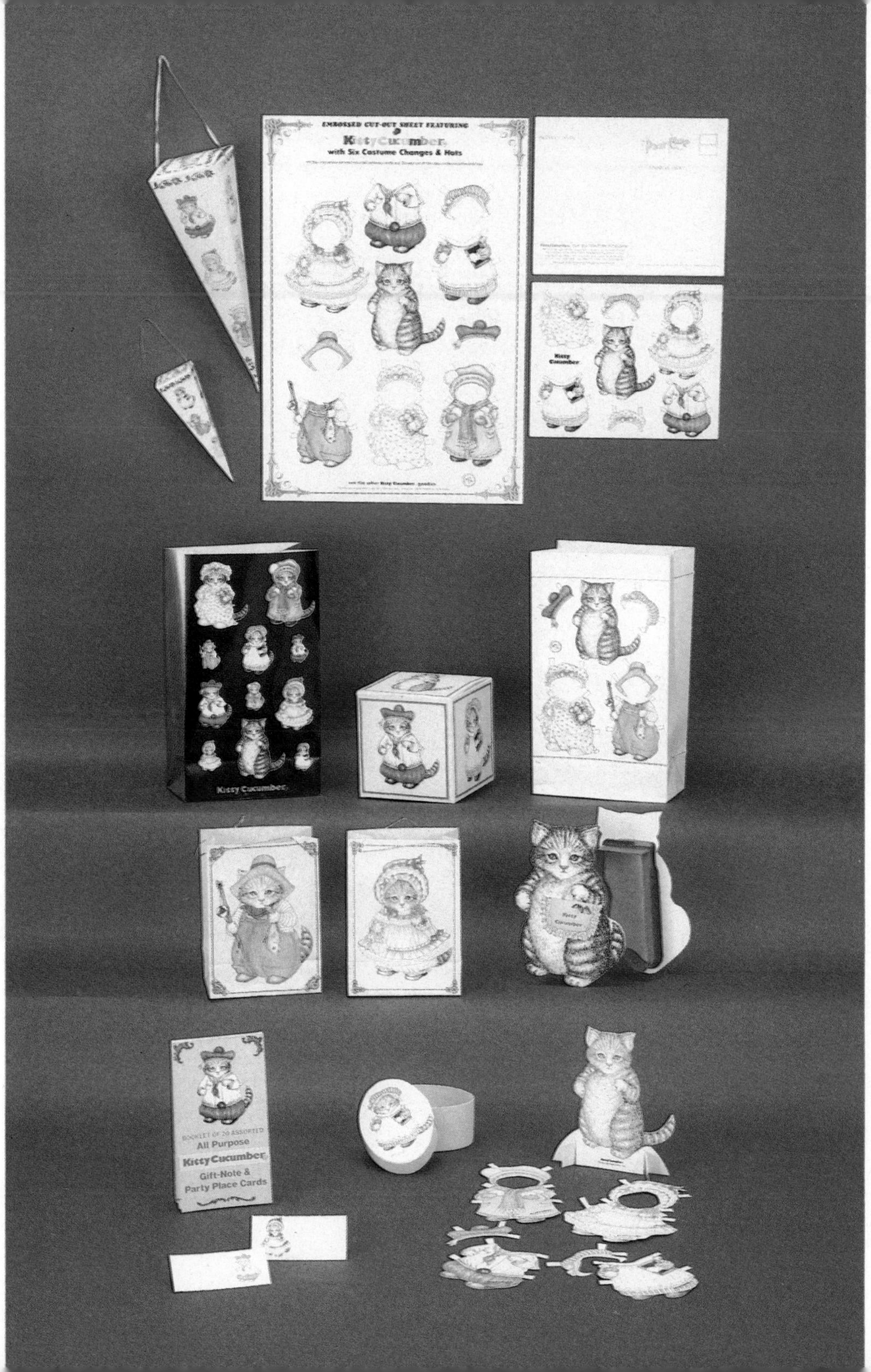

PARTY FAVOR and cat clicker with moving eyes and tongue. Each, 83-A

KITTY CUCUMBER™ BOOKS, CONTAINERS & PAPERDOLLS: 9½″ cornucopia container. (21311); 5″ mini cornucopia. (30602); 10½″x15″ embossed paperdoll sheet. (30243); 6″x8″ jumbo paperdoll postcard (pkg. of 12). (30441); 9½″ varnished gift bag. (30410); 4″ varnished cube gift box. (40528); 9½″ varnished paperdoll gift bag. (40537); 5½″ varnished shopping bag (6 dif.). (21309); 3″x5″ die-cut box. (40529); 5½″x3″ booklet of 20 place cards. (30413); 2½″x3″ oval wood box (6 dif.). (40584); 5½″ paperdoll with six costumes. (21304)
83-See price information in "Source List."

KITTY CUCUMBER™ PAPER GOODS: 7″ fold-out greeting card with envelope. (30477); 3″ Kitty Cucumber™ ornament/tie-ons with gold strings (set of 6) (21306); 3″ ornament/tie-ons with gold strings (set of 6). (30521); Pkg. of three sheets, Kitty & Friends pressure-sensitive seals. (30524); Pkg. of three sheets, Kitty Cucumber™ pressure-sensitive seals. (21312); 10″ Kitty & Friends card with envelope. (30523); 10″ Kitty Cucumber™ card with envelope. (21310); 2″ Kitty Cucumber™ note/tags (pkg. of 12). (40619); 2″ Kitty & Friends note/tags (pkg. of 12). (30526); 2″ Kitty Cucumber™ gift/notes with envelope. (21307); 3½″ die-cut gift tags with gold strings (pkg. of 12). (40535); 3″ Kitty Cucumber™ party toothpicks (pkg. of 12). (40690); 1½″ Mini Kitty Cucumber™ paper dolls. (30409). 83-See price information in "Source List."

ROLY-POLY CAT tin opens to store catnip or small treasures. 3½″ high. 83-F

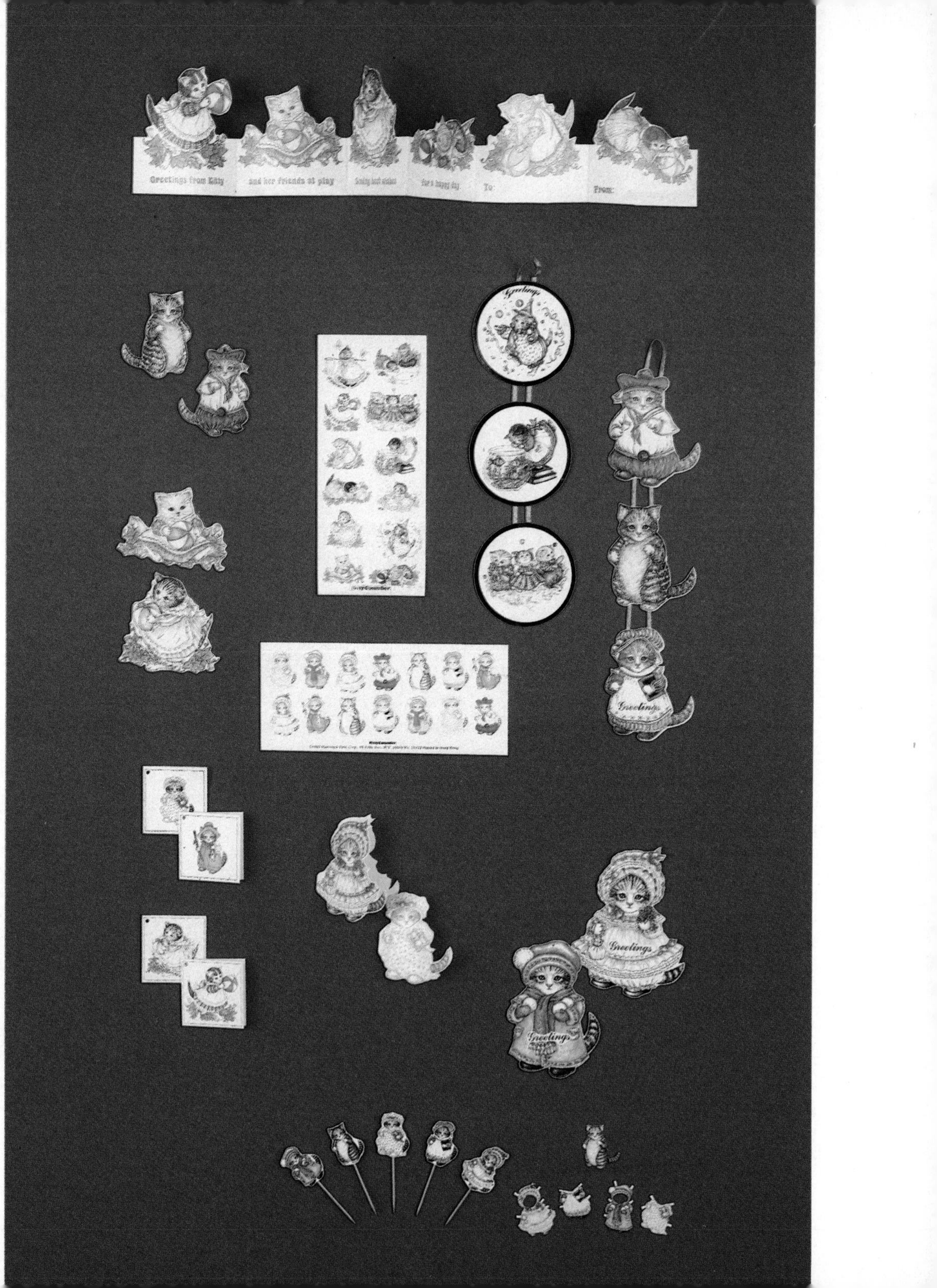

SLEEPING CAT in terra cotta for indoors or out—in the garden, patio, flower bed or window seat. 11″Wx5″H. (32-65094) 5-C

LIMITED EDITION collector plate, part of a numbered edition of 10,000, by photographer Robert Pearcy. 8½″ diameter, banded in gold. 41-C

TERRA COTTA PLANT HOLDERS. Carefully glazed inside so they won't lose a drop of water. 7″L or 6″H. (G676981) Set of 3, 8NH-B

FRENCH SCARE CAT. Glittering marble eyes and distinctive features help protect fruit trees and vegetable gardens from marauding birds, rabbits or other nibblers. Hang scare cat from a tree or nail to a fence. All metal. 14″Wx6½″H. (32-65359) 5-B

"LOVE IS A HAPPY CAT." A wise and whimsical treasury of knowledge about how and why cats behave the way they do. Eighty-seven cartoons illustrate this book by Dr. Michael W. Fox. 89-A

"Buy it. Read it. Give it. Don't miss this book." CAT FANCY MAGAZINE
LOVE IS A HAPPY CAT
Dr. Michael W. Fox
author of UNDERSTANDING YOUR CAT
For all ages—the most original cat care and behavior book ever created. "Genuinely charming and informative, with a cartoon cat-character that outcutes Garfield." PUBLISHERS WEEKLY
Cartoons by Harry Gans
Love is understanding that, like you, we often get carried away by our instincts.


DECORATIVE PILLOWS in assorted "Fabulous Felines" patterns. Natural 100% cotton covers; plump polyester cotton fill. Approx. 10″x12″ (G568170B) Each, 8-A; two, 8OV-B

"THE WHITE CAT" is a life-size purse that converts to a life-like hand puppet. The fabric is completely stitched with thread, and then hundreds of individual threads are added by hand to create the "fur." 48-P

2 PURSES IN 1. Thousands of threads are hand-sewn to create this multicolor life-size cat purse. It's two purses in one—the body being a large purse with a zipper hidden at the top, and the tail a smaller purse for make-up, keys, etc. 48-P

PURSE & PUPPET. This life-size cat purse is totally stitched to create its multi-color stripes. Its tail makes a comfortable shoulder strap, and this puss becomes a puppet by unzipping its back and putting your hand inside. 48-N

JIGSAW PUZZLES. You can while away the hours piecing together these three fetching felines.

"NAME THAT TUNE." 1000 pieces. 64-A

"PEEK-A-BOO." 1000 pieces. 64-A

"GREAT EXPECTATIONS." 551 pieces. 64-A

"ABC IN KITTEN LAND." A reproduction of an antique original that flops to become "ABC in Puppyland." 83-A

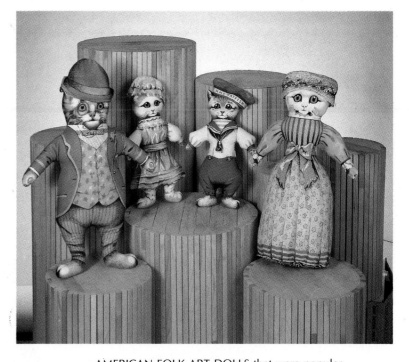

AMERICAN FOLK ART DOLLS that were popular in the 1800's. These antique reproductions are hand printed on natural fabrics filled with natural fibers. Little Miss Tabby Cat in pinafore and bonnet with her Sailor Boy Friend, 9½" tall (73) the pair, 9-B; Mr. and Mrs. Top Cat, 13" tall (737) the pair, 9-C

PRINT TURTLENECKS. Cat and mouse design on shirts of 60% cotton, 40% polyester. SML. (X2986-13). 76-C

"SPATSVILLE 'WHISKERS' COLLECTION." Matching T-shirts and accessories for the whole family. Handscreened cats have sewn-in whiskers that appear to be real. From 102A through 102F.

HAND STENCILED LAMP. Cranberry colored heavy wood base. Delicately pierced shade with velvet trim. UL listed. 16″ high. (8463) 57-J

SAFETY HALTER. Double strap protects against neck strain. Cat can't wiggle free. Riveted saddle leather. Chest strap adjusts to 18", neck to 14". (G365643) 8HH-A

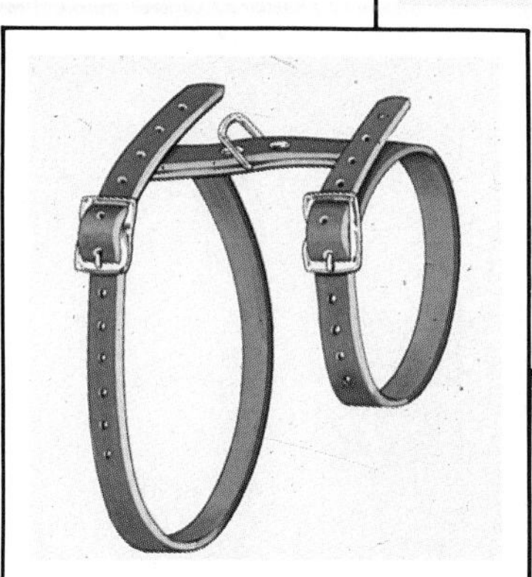

"EASYTHRU," the "pet-friendly door." A see-through panel lets timid pets check if the coast is clear. Opens safely in both directions with a gentle push. Closes automatically; can be locked. Easy to install. 84-H

"THE CITY CAT. How to Live Healthily and Happily with Your Indoor Pet." Can a cat be really happy indoors? Yes, says Roz Riddle, co-owner of Fabulous Felines, a Manhattan shop; and she tells you how. 20 black and white photos, 21 drawings. 176 pages. 5½"x8¼". 65-B

"KITTI-POTTI" has charcoal air filter for freshness. The top fits inside the bottom to make it spray proof. 7" diameter hole is just right for all cats. Beige, 22Lx16Wx18"H. (9422400) 27-D; charcoal filter replacements available. Metal screen cover to protect the filter from the cat's curiosity not included. Screen: (9422492) 27-A

THE BEAST BAG looks like a general purpose carry-on, enables you to carry a quiet pet, unnoticed. Use a tote or shoulder bag. Light-weight, water repellent. Soft sides permit you to comfort cat en route. Vet approved. Meets airline specs for in-cabin travel. Base size 16"x9". Weight: 1 lb. Colors: teal, terra cotta or tan. 26-E

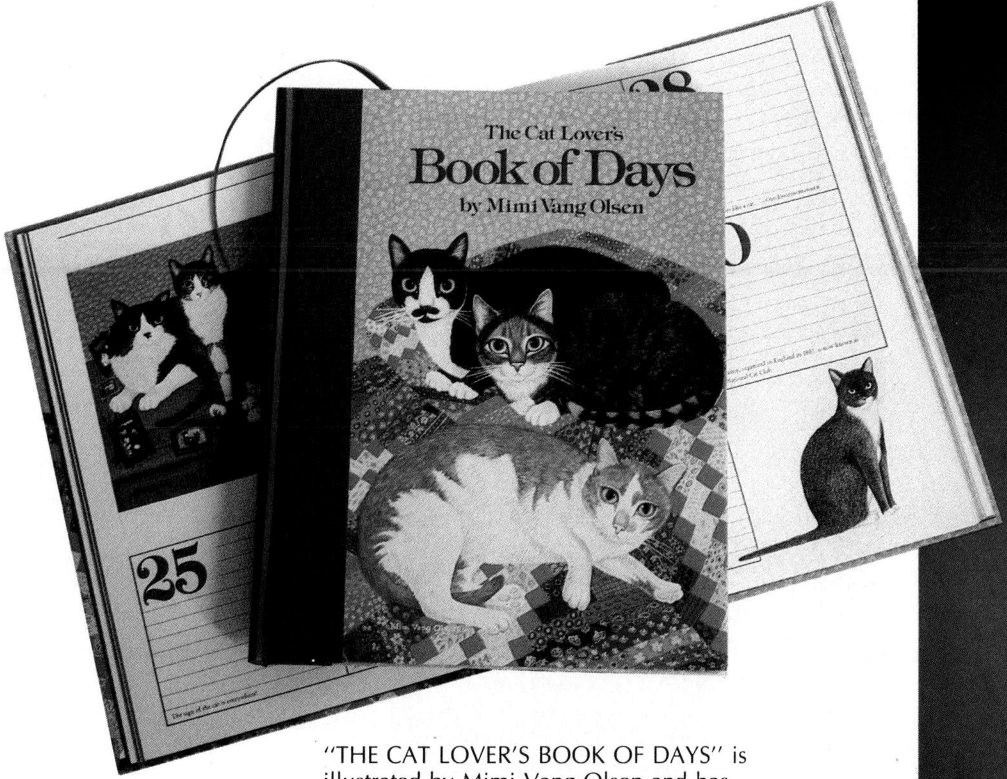

"THE CAT LOVER'S BOOK OF DAYS" is illustrated by Mimi Vang Olsen and has text by Ronnie Leonards. Here's a daily reminder or birthday book, profusely illustrated with drawings and paintings of cats, and with a cat-oriented fact or thought for each day of the year. 56-B

BREAKFAST CAT STONEWARE by Susan Wrightsman of Lempster Pottery. A 3-pc. place setting designed especially for children. 16-C

T-SHIRT AND WRAP SKIRT of hand screened cotton fabric. Siamese Brown ink on natural, from cat drawings by Marilyn Coon. T-shirt is 50/50 combed cotton and polyester, 77-A; wrap skirt is hand washable 100% cotton, S-M-L, 77-E. "Cats" fabric, 48" wide, also available by the yard. 77-B

CAT ROCKS. Hand selected rocks painted as cats to ornament any room. Choice of eye color may be specified: yellow, brown, blue or green. Small (3″), 91-B; medium (5″), 91-B; large (8″), 91-C

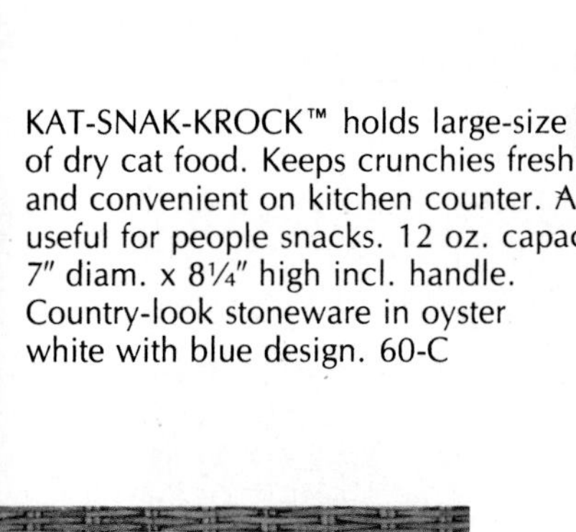

KAT-SNAK-KROCK™ holds large-size box of dry cat food. Keeps crunchies fresh and convenient on kitchen counter. Also useful for people snacks. 12 oz. capacity, 7″ diam. x 8¼″ high incl. handle. Country-look stoneware in oyster white with blue design. 60-C

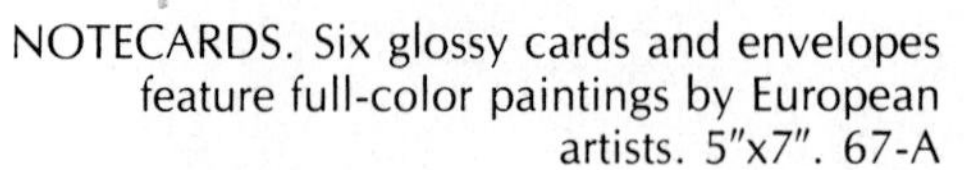

NOTECARDS. Six glossy cards and envelopes feature full-color paintings by European artists. 5″x7″. 67-A

LUV·A·KAT KLOCK™ is made from a dinner plate of country-look stoneware in oyster white, hand stenciled in blue. Glazed finish. Quartz clock movement with sweep second hand runs for a year or more on one battery. 10¼″ diameter. 60-D

PORCELAIN "MANEKI-NEKO" is 5½" high and has gold accents. 70-B

WINDSOCK. 52" long. Made of parachute silk/nylon and available in a variety of colors. 70-C

THE BECKONING CAT. "Maneki-Neko" is the heroic cat of Japanese folk literature who killed a snake, fought off thieves, etc. to save a princess. It is the popular good luck figure of Japan, and is used by shop-keepers there to attract "nice people." The Beckoning Cat is also the name of a shop in Evanston, Illinois, many of whose items are shown on this and other pages.

PORCELAIN PILLOW from Thailand. Blue and white carp decoration. May be used as a doorstop. 70-D

PORCELAIN CAT from Thailand is 12″ high. Blue and white decoration includes bow around neck. 70-E

SMALL "MANEKI-NEKO'S" on pillows. In black or white. 1¼″ high: 70-A. 3″ high: 70-A

PAPIER-MACHE "MANEKI-NEKO'S." Brightly painted in sizes 6″ to 12″ high. 70-A to C

POTTERY CATS from Mexico. Hand painted with nature motifs. 26″ tall. 70-F

MUG; No-Spill Mug; Round Guys Buttons; Keychains; Little Guys Pads; Small Composition Books; Medium Composition Books; Post-It Notes. Each, 92-A

CATMAN CAPE TOWEL AND PUPPET MITT WASHCLOTH. Double-sided terry, cotton trim, machine embroidered detailing. Towel, 45″ square. Mitt, 10″x7½″ (145). The set, 24-D. Part of The Cat Companion Collection.™

CERAMIC PLANTER can be a dinner table centerpiece. Blanket colors are also available in Sunflower Yellow, Light Green or Pink. Turquoise eyes. Hand painted by "Lisa." Triple-fired. Each piece is signed by the artist. 10″H, base 9¼″Wx7½″ deep; 14¾″ handle to handle. Plant not included. (187) 24-G. Part of The Cat Companion Collection.™

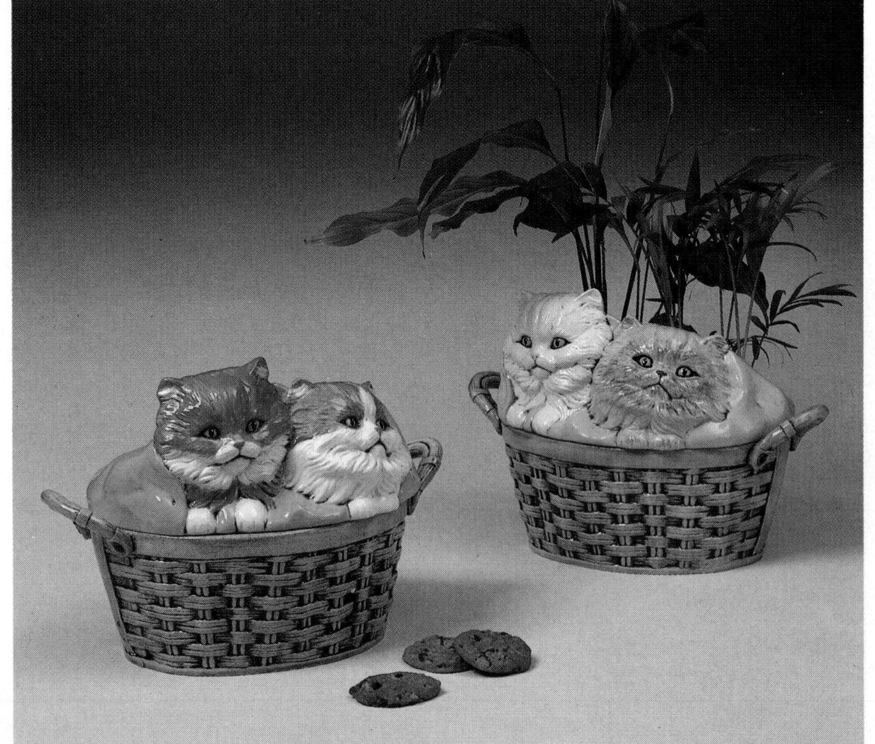

CATMAN CAPE TOWEL AND PUPPET MITT WASHCLOTH. Double-sided terry, cotton trim, machine embroidered detailing. Towel, 45″ square. Mitt, 10″x7½″ (145) The set, 24-D Part of The Cat Companion Collection.™

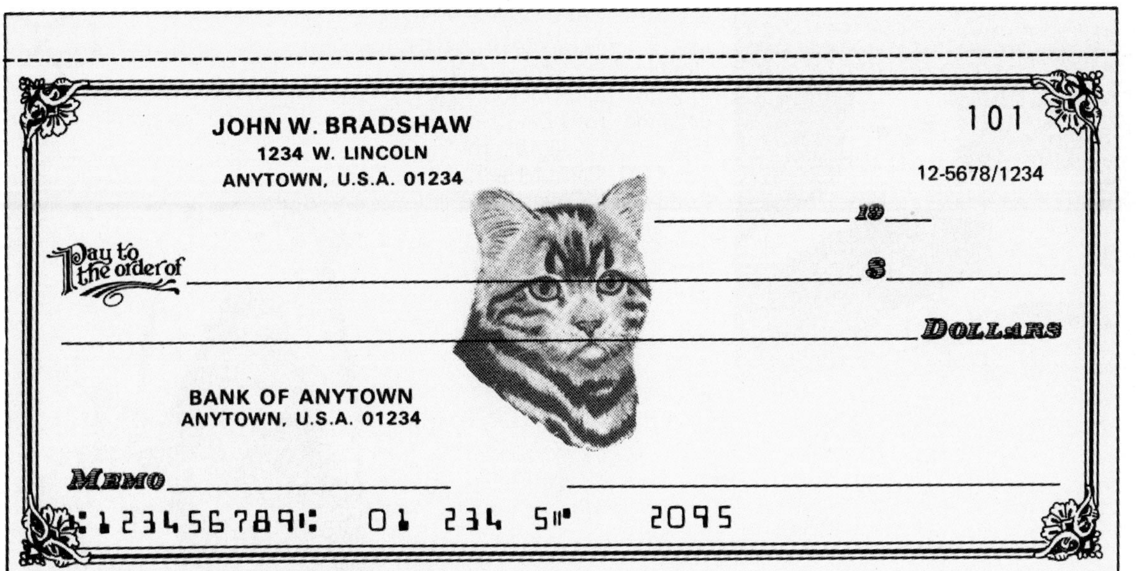

JOHN W. BRADSHAW
1234 W. LINCOLN
ANYTOWN, U.S.A. 01234

101

12-5678/1234

19

Pay to the order of ________ $

DOLLARS

BANK OF ANYTOWN
ANYTOWN, U.S.A. 01234

MEMO

⑆123456789⑆ 01 234 5⑈ 2095

CAT-PERSONALIZED CHECKS. These finely detailed "Special Interest Checks" are acceptable for use with your account at any bank. They are created by a nation-wide supplier of bank forms. Printed on a choice of three backgrounds: Sporty Denim, Distinctive Parchment, or Sparkling White. Select your design from a wide variety of cat breeds, or order custom checks made with your photo or drawing of your pet. Your original is returned unharmed. 200 checks, 81-A; custom checks, 81-C for the first order, 81-A thereafter. Larger 3-to-page business checks are also available.

TWO BY PAUL GALLICO. "The Silent Miaow", a manual for kittens, strays, and homeless cats. Copyright © 1964 by Paul W. Gallico and Suzanne Szasz. Used by permission of Crown Publishers, Inc. 109-A; "Honorable Cat". Copyright © 1972 by Paul Gallico and Mathemata Anstalt. Used by permission of Crown Publishers, Inc. 93-A.

The Silent Miaow
a manual for kittens, strays, and homeless cats
Translated from the Feline
by PAUL GALLIC
Picture Story
by SUZANNE SZASZ

THREE WEDGWOOD PAIRS of cat plates. Cat Collectors is the U.S. distributor. The ones pictured are by artist John Mould. Issue price: 73-E per plate; plates must be purchased in pairs.

PET GRAVE MARKER KIT. Mark your pet's burial place with beauty and dignity. The kit contains a 6x6x2″ brushed stainless steel marker, and materials that enable you to write a personal message and imbed a photo. The marker rests well-anchored and flush with the ground for safe grass cutting. 53-D

PET MONUMENT. A final tribute to a loving and devoted companion. 4″ thick x 8″ x 16″ first quality grey granite memorial. Other sizes and pet emblems available. 11-E

A SONG FOR YOUR CAT. "Petsong" is a custom-composed song on a 2-to-2½-minute cassette tape (the original recording). It is performed with vocals and full instrumentation. Song is written according to the information you send along with your order. It attempts to capture the personality and unique traits of your pet. With the tape, you receive a printed copy of the lyrics. Choice of Folk, Country or Rock style music; other styles on special request. Composer is Dennis Knick. 7-B

VIDEO CATS. Video cassettes for the whole family to enjoy: "Waldo Kitty," Vol. I. 48 Min.; "Peter No-Tail" (Children's Video Library). Features the voices of Ken Berry, Dom De Luise, Richard Kline, Tina Louise, Larry Storch, June Lockhart and William Schallert. 82 Min.; "Shinebone Alley." The Broadway show expanded into an animated feature. Features Carol Channing. Rated G. 83 Min.; "The Cat from Outer Space" (Walt Disney). Stars Ken Berry, Sandy Duncan. 103 Min. "Puss'n Boots." The children's classic. 14-C to 14-F

"CLASSICAL CATS." This London® record features music inspired by cats. Composers include Chopin, Scarlatti, Ravel, Prokofiev, Copland, and others. 10-A

THERMOMETER/MAGNET sticks to refrigerator, file cabinet, etc. Fahrenheit and Celsius. (J567552) 8HH-A

GARFIELD'S AN ANGEL to dangle from your tree. Artplas, 3" high. (J868653) 8-A. Hang this or another favorite ornament on the revolving musical stand. Wind it up and the brass hanger revolves to "Deck the Halls." Artplas, 8"x4" diameter. (J868679) 8A-B

CATCARDS. A book of 24 humorous postcards by illustrator, Victoria Chess, includes Mikhail Baryshnicat, Catman & Robin, and Joseph & His Cat of Many Colors. 97-A

COFFEE COZY or blender cover of insulated cotton and polyester. Hand washable. 16″ tall, 11″ wide. (H602V) 88-B

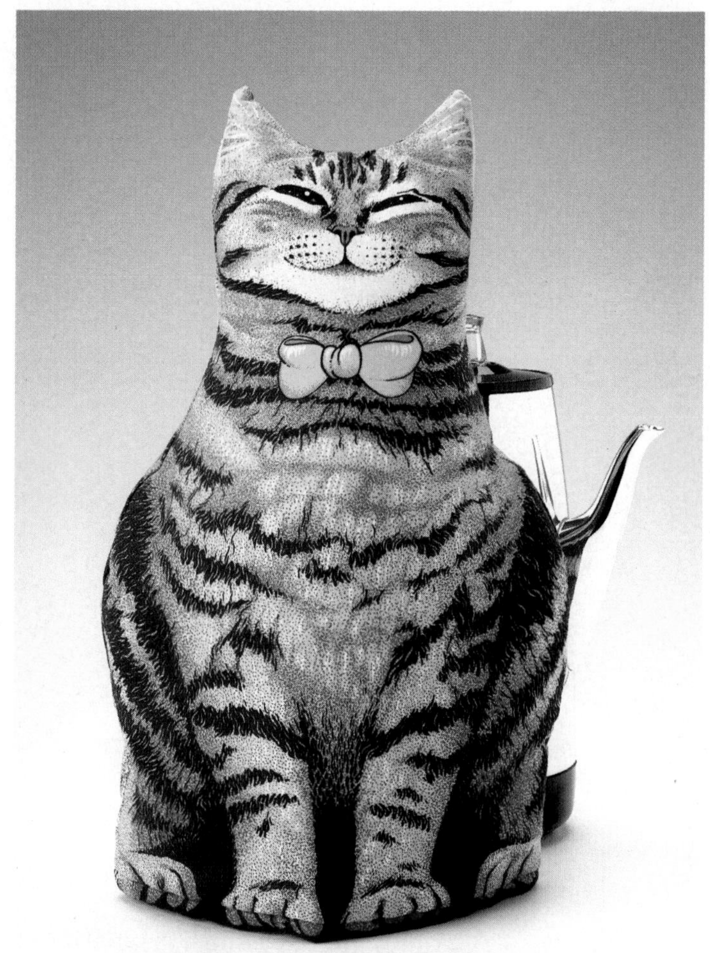

CHRISTMAS ORNAMENT can also be a gift. Semi- or-precious stones. Gemstones can be set as removable pierced earrings. Approx. 5½"x6½". 2-L

YOUR CAT ON BROOCH OR LOCKET, painted in miniature. Approx. 1¼"x1¾". 2-M. 22 karat hand crafted gold frame additional.

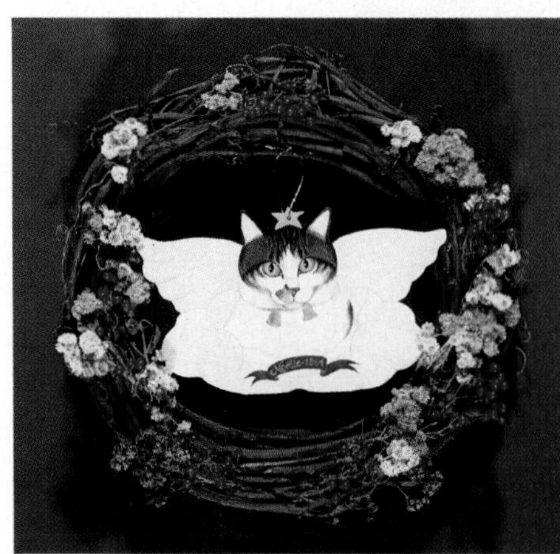

CHRISTMAS CAT on pine wood, polyurethaned. Approx. 9"x5". 2-K. Wreath can be included at additional cost.

WITCHES' WARES. A few of the hundreds of occult items carried by *Magickal Childe* (formerly *The Warlock Shop)* in New York City.

CAT CANDLES. Red or black. 3½″ high. 46-A

CAT SUN SIGNS by Vivian Buchan. 46-A

CATSIGNS. A lunar guide for cats and their owners. 46-A

SIX-CAT CANDLEHOLDER. Made of hand painted ceramic. $3\frac{1}{4}''$ tall x$5\frac{3}{4}''$ diameter. Candle not included. (H717710) 8ROG-B

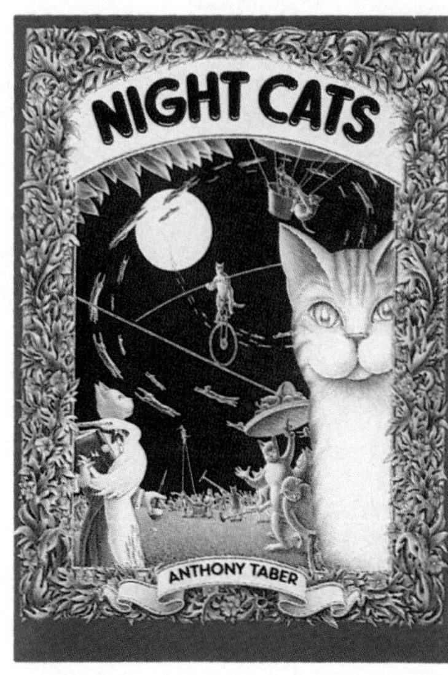


"NIGHT CATS." *New Yorker* artist Anthony Taber shows how cats spend their nights in dramatic pen-and-ink drawings. Paperback. 49-A

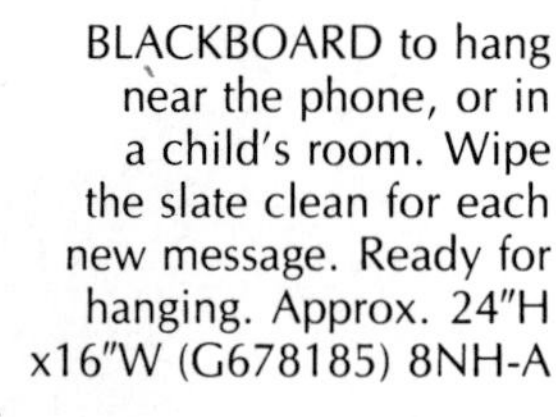

BLACKBOARD to hang near the phone, or in a child's room. Wipe the slate clean for each new message. Ready for hanging. Approx. 24"H x16"W (G678185) 8NH-A

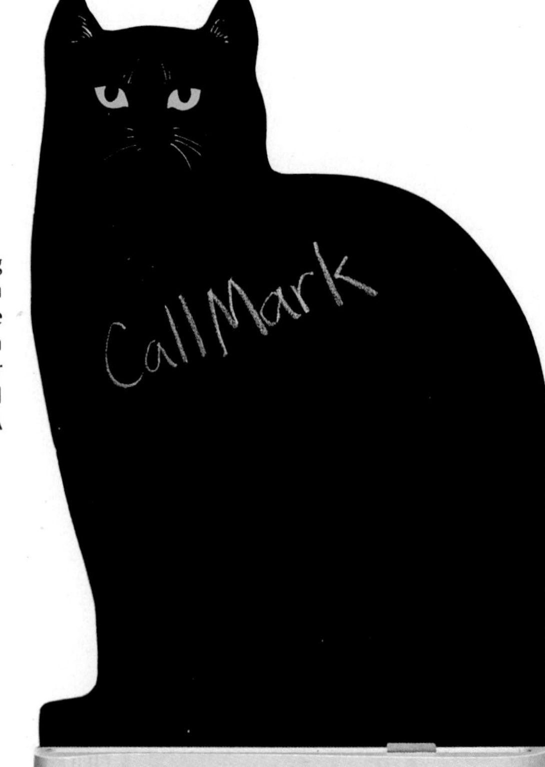


T-SHIRTS. Cotton/poly T-shirt displays unusual "Cats" design. Adult sizes only: S-M-L. White design on navy. (8464) 57-A

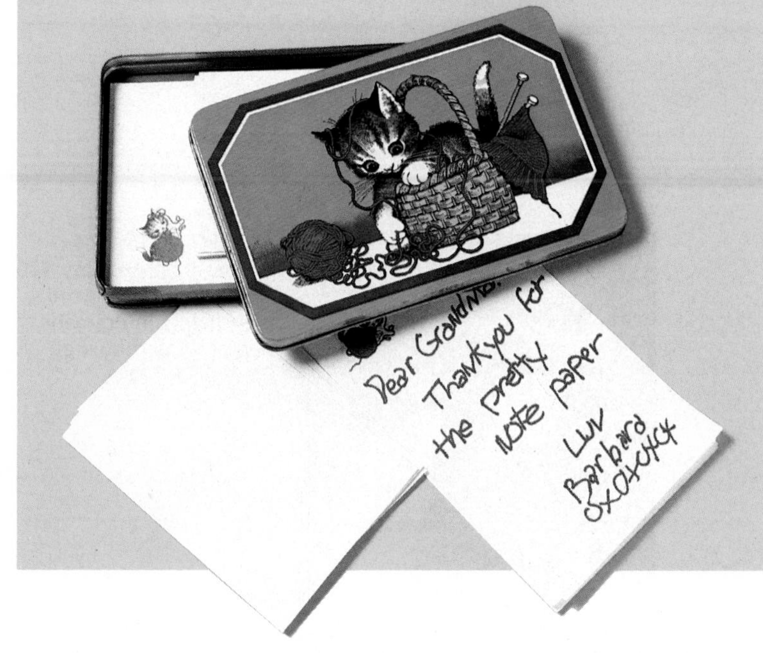


STATIONERY IN A TIN. Notepaper, 4½"x7½", has a playful kitten in the corner. Envelopes included. Tin is reusable. (G570358) 8OV-A

WIND CHIME. Mama and ten kittens. High fired ceramic, hand painted. 6½"Wx26"L. (G551110) 8HH-A

CAST IRON BANK. A heavy guard for your coins. Matte finish. About 8" tall. (JT17884) 8OV-A

CATS ON A YELLOW GRID. Ceramic mugs. 45-A

CATS AT THE SHORE on porcelain plate sets and matching mugs. 9″ diameter plates (J771238) Set of 4, 8-E. 10 oz. mugs. (J771246) 8HA-C

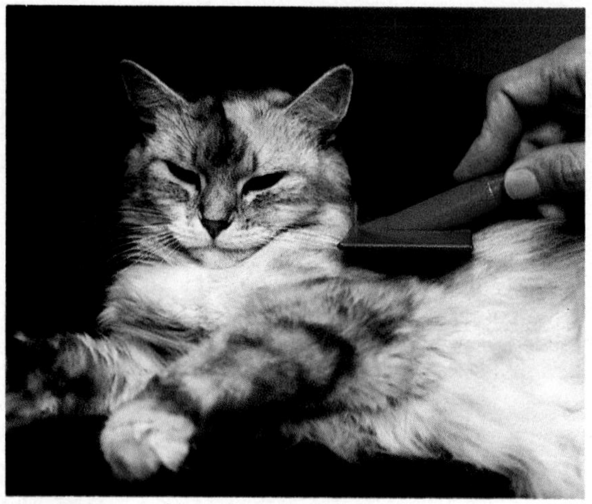

YOUR CAT'S FUR COMBINGS HANDSPUN INTO YARN. Jean Warholic will spin the combings into 2-ply yarn for you to knit, crochet or weave into a soft scarf, hat or vest, depending on the quantity you provide. Jean uses the undercoat combings only, so color depends on that. Min. order, one ounce. There are approx. 60 yards to the ounce of medium yarn (like sportweight); a finer yarn (like baby yarn) yields about 80 yards. No samples. Per ounce, 100-A

ANITRA FRAZIER, author of "The Natural Cat," with Big Purr. Frazier conducts Anitra Cat Grooming Plus, a worldwide phone and mail consultation service dealing with behavioral problems, general care and nutrition. She emphasizes a holistic, natural approach. For New York City clients, she includes grooming and consultations in the cats' own homes.

See Source listing No. 4.

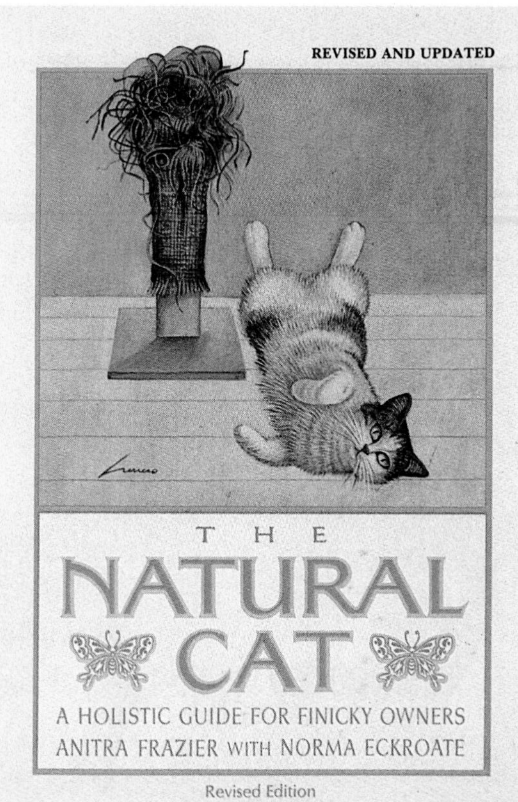


"THE NATURAL CAT: A Holistic Guide for Finicky Owners" by Anitra Frazier. This reference book takes the natural approach emphasizing an ounce of prevention. Subjects include communication, guiding behavior patterns, building health, and pampering the elderly or ailing cat. Line drawings. 1983. Revised edition. 96-A

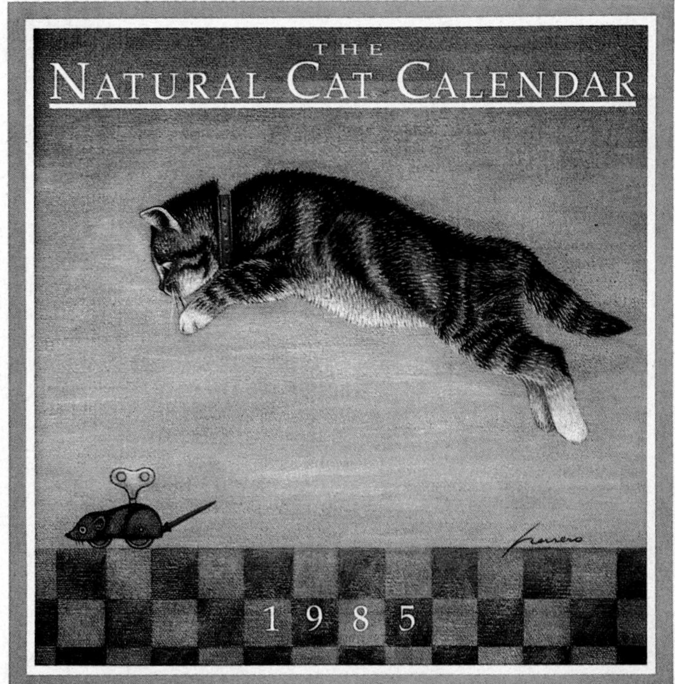


"THE NATURAL CAT CALENDAR." Original paintings by Lowell Herrero depicting the many moods of our feline companions, along with helpful tips for cat care. Published yearly (1986 now avail.). 96-A

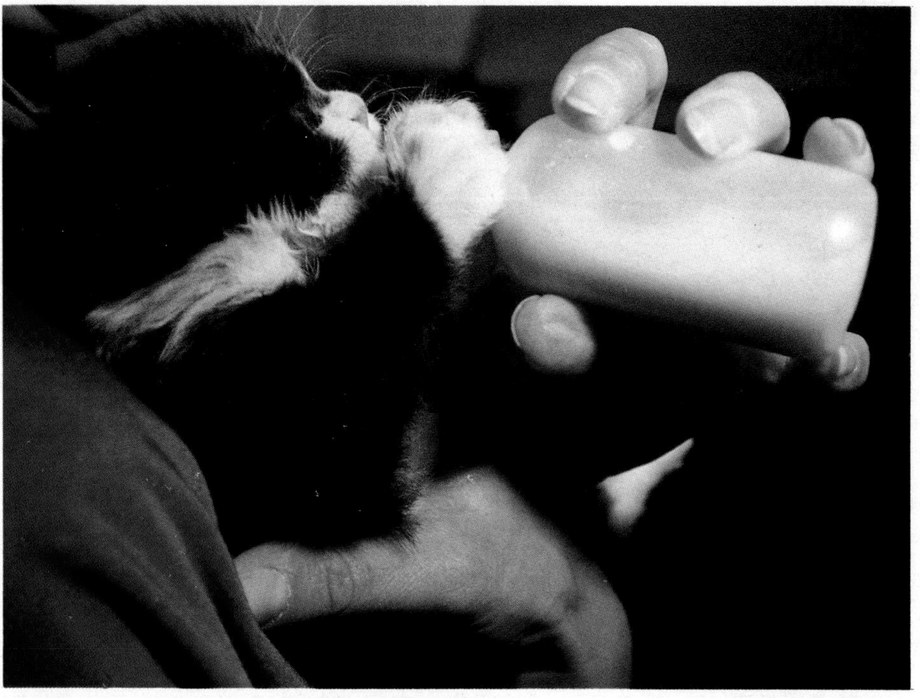

CAT BRASSES. Ornaments such as these have been used on horse harnesses since the eighteenth century. They may be used as pendants or wall ornaments as well. Approx. 3″ diameter. 42-A

ORPHAN KITTEN NURSING BOTTLES. Feed just one orphan, or a litter of six all at once. Experts say that kittens develop more favorably when nursing together rather than singly; and of course the saving in care-time is considerable. One dozen, 20-A

SWEATER GRAPHICS. Night cat perched on front and sleeves of this intarsia knit, full turtleneck in washable acrylic. Red/black. S (6-8), M (10-12) L (14-16). (G252486) 8CC-D

A WAY TO REMEMBER your cat. Personalized memorials commemorate the life of your cat in these ink and watercolor documents, reminiscent of Early American fracturs. Animal portraitist, Susan Gray, includes epitaphs, animal prayers, poetry, or your own personal sentiments in the design. Approx. 10″x12″ 2-L

MUSIC BOX is also a candy dish. Hand painted porcelain. Removable lid. Wind it up and it plays "Memories" from the Broadway show "Cats." (5572842) 8OV-B

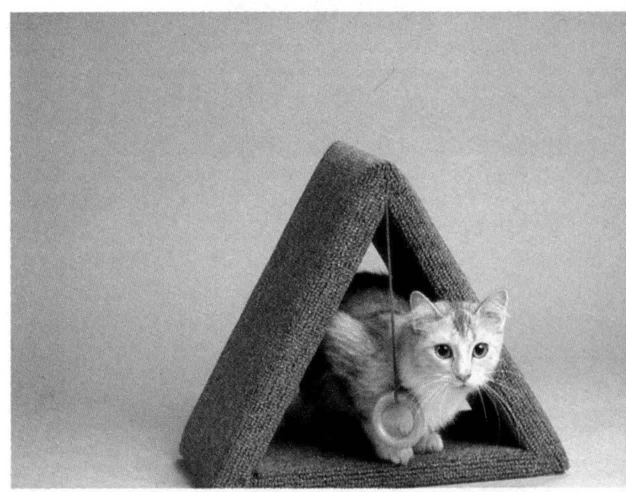

"CATHY" PORCELAIN features the same wide-eyed feline against different colored backgrounds. Set includes one each of blue, deep rose, cinnamon and lustrous black. High-fired to enjoy every day. (39783) Four 7½" plates, 58-C; (39793) Four 10 oz. mugs, 58PP-C

TEDDY AND KITTY NEEDLEPOINT picture by Linda K. Powell, to stitch yourself. "Purr-fect Pals" kit includes everything except the mat. Frame separate. 14"x11". (617863) 58S-C; 18"x15" wood frame. (961983) 58S-B

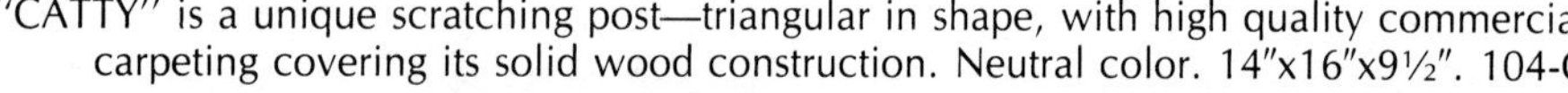

"CATTY" is a unique scratching post—triangular in shape, with high quality commercial carpeting covering its solid wood construction. Neutral color. 14"x16"x9½". 104-C

SUNCATCHER/MOBILE. Scandinavian design. 6″x8″. Navy. (8430) 57-A

KITTY CUCUMBER™ TIN BUCKET with 40 marbles. Bucket is 3¼″. (30528) 83-See price information in "Source List."

GREETING CARDS by illustrator Marilyn Hafner. 4¾″x7″. Each, 63-A

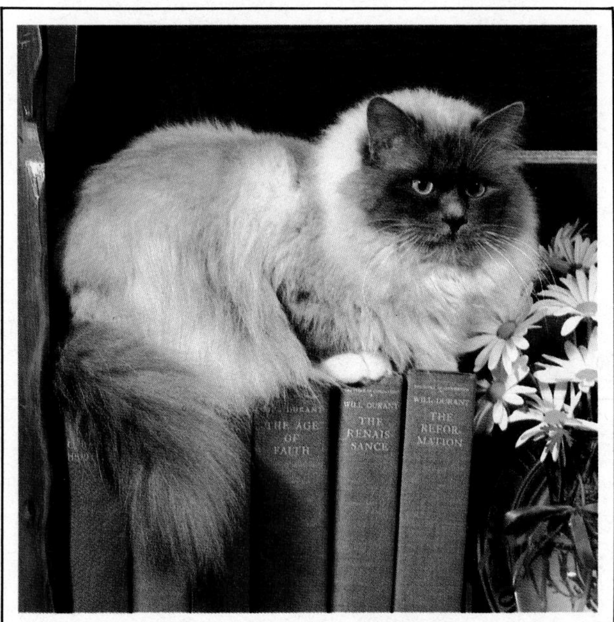


"THE CAT BOOK CENTER" stocks fiction and nonfiction pertaining to cats, mostly out-of-print (used, but in good condition). Mrs. Zeehandelaar, who owns and operates this exclusively mail-order service, also imports cat books from England, Germany and France. She provides a search service as well, gratis. Sorry, no juveniles. 123-A

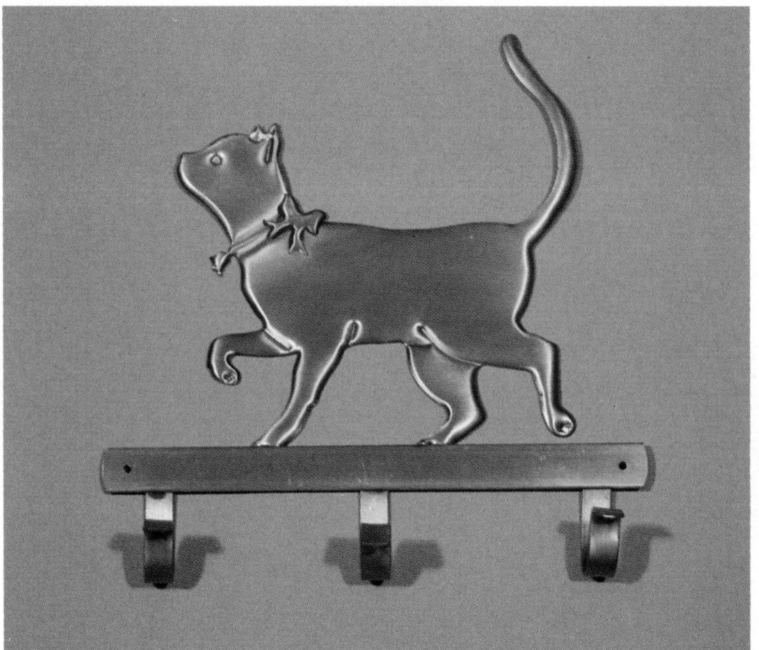

BRASS HOOKS. Solid brass and copper design features either two or three hooks. Includes hanging hardware. 10"x10½". 3 hooks, (8449) 57-B; 2 hooks, (8450) 57-B

KITTY TAPE DISPENSER. Takahashi's ceramic cat has multicolored floral & cat design. 3"x5". Tape not included. (8477) 57-A

ANDERSON'S CAT FURNITURE. The "Castle" is covered with top quality carpet and lined with fresh catnip. 75-K

GIFTWRAP PACK. Assortment of cat wrapping paper. Two sheets each of three designs. 12″x12″. (8432) 57-A

STICKER PACK. Cats and kittens galore in this full-color assortment. Many shapes and sizes. (8439) Pack, 57-A

MOUSE DISH for feeding a cat. Shaped like a mouse with compartments for food and water. White, light blue or cream colored. Handmade by Lilly Butcher. 75-A

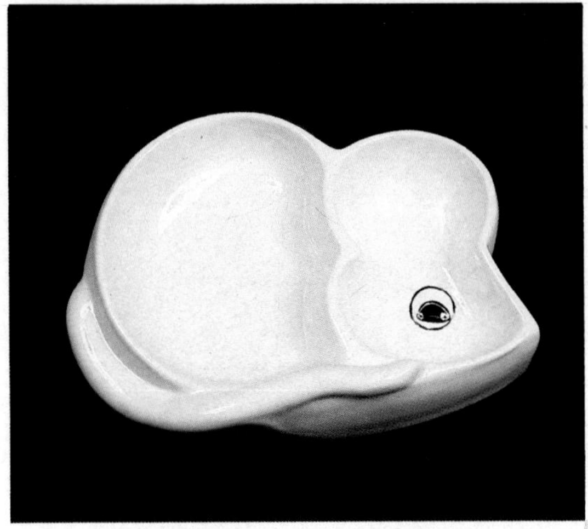

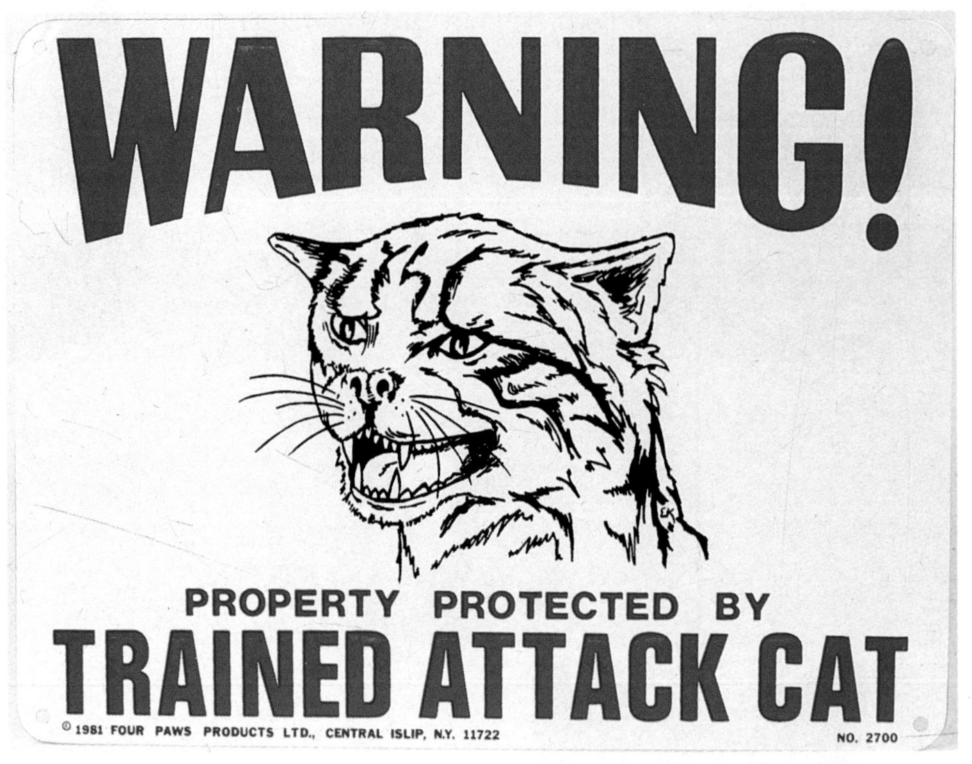
WARNING!
PROPERTY PROTECTED BY
TRAINED ATTACK CAT
© 1981 FOUR PAWS PRODUCTS LTD., CENTRAL ISLIP, N.Y. 11722
NO. 2700

WARNING SIGN. Non-rust metal. For indoors or out. 75-A

FUR MICE look and feel real. Fun for the mouse-less cat. Each, 75-A

MASKS. Handmade with a traditional papier-mache process. To wear or hang on the wall. (151, Black; 152, Tabby; 153, White) 24-C; "Le Bandit" is a mask-on-a-stick constructed of heavy paper. (154) 24-A

THE CAT COMPANION COLLECTION™
This mail-order collection of cat theme objects grew out of Alice Pasqualetti's Cat Companion Care, an in-your-home cat sitting service. Mrs. Pasqualetti observed that many clients expressed their love of cat friends in fine quality artwork, jewelry and clothing. So, with her husband Roy, she began a world-wide search for unusual, high quality items. Ninety-five percent of the Collection is now commissioned solely for the Pasqualettis. Some of these objects are shown here, others throughout this book.

STAINED GLASS PANEL by Terry Nixon. Opalescent Silver Tabby design outlined with copper and framed by a band of amber glass; hand-rubbed solid oak frame. 23¾″x19″. (146) 24-M

SOLID BRASS BED for one or two cats. Easy to assemble. 21″ deep x 31″ wide x 16″ overall height. (147) 24-K. White queen size "Montclair" pillow and sham are of washable polyester satin. (150) 24-K. Cat not included.

SOAP SCULPTURES to use. Pure, mild glycerine soap from handmade molds. 4¼″H. Yellow jasmine-scented (165); green pine-scented (166); red sandalwood-scented (167); or package of 3 assorted (167a). 24-A

TAFFY reclines on a queen size patchwork pillow designed by Terrie Milestone Soldavini. Removable pillow cover with envelope opening. Hand-wash or dry clean. (149) 24-K.

"THE CAT MADE ME BUY IT!" A collection of cats who sold yesterday's products. 116 full-color illustrations show ads, signs, labels, packages, magazine covers and more that helped sell products in the pre-television era between the late 1800's and the 1940's. 8½"x11". 96 pages. Copyright © 1984 by Alice L. Muncaster and Ellen Yanow. Used by permission of Crown Publishers, Inc. 93-A

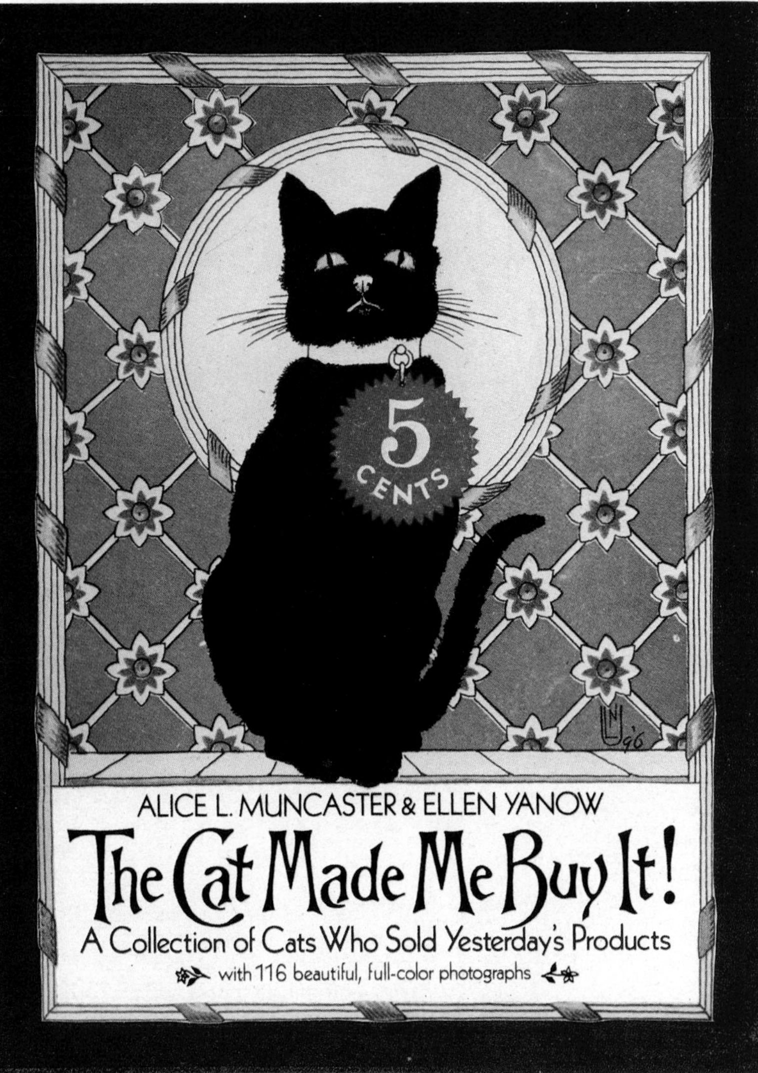


"SNOWING" MUSIC BOX. Glass encased holiday figurine on a wood base. Tip it over to start the snowflakes swirling. Christmas Kitty plays "Winter Wonderland." 5½" tall. (G569517B) 8OV-B

JAPANESE PORCELAIN. Hand painted butterflies and flowers lend a pastoral feeling. 9¼" long. (J771642) 8HA-D

CAT WINDCHIMES. Six ceramic cats turn and tinkle musically in any breeze. 12″ high. (J574343) 8HH-A

MINIATURES. Handcrafted and handpainted metal cats for your dollhouse or elsewhere. Eight different items include a kitty in a litter box. Each, 43-A

BRASS CAT with antiqued verdigris finish is displayed on a mahogany wood base. 4x3x7″. (G793802) 8HA-E

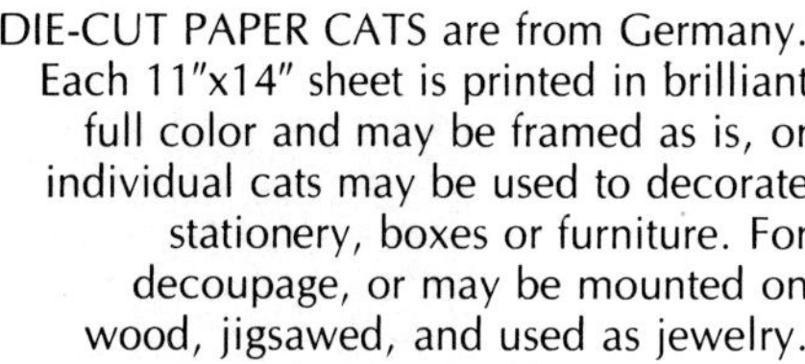

DIE-CUT PAPER CATS are from Germany. Each 11″x14″ sheet is printed in brilliant full color and may be framed as is, or individual cats may be used to decorate stationery, boxes or furniture. For decoupage, or may be mounted on wood, jigsawed, and used as jewelry.

KIDDIECATS. 72 die-cut kittens. 79-A

CATS IN COSTUME. 48 figures include sailors and Spanish dancers. 79-A

CATS & DOGS. 21 die-cut figures. 79-A

CUDDLY KITTENS. 16 larger die-cut figures, some with other animal friends. 79-A

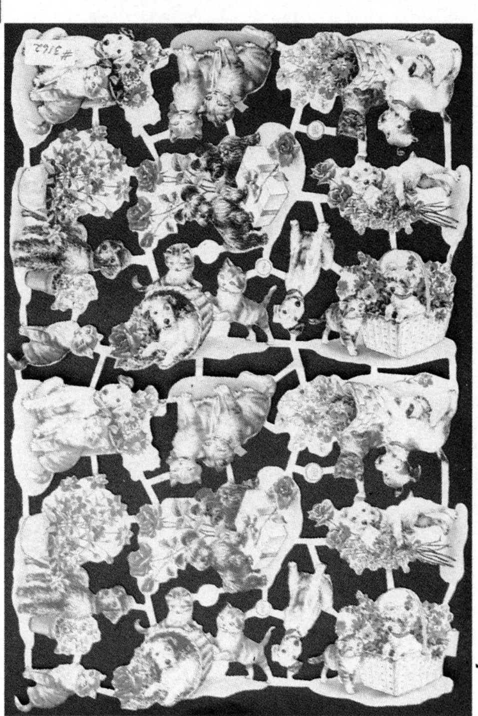

LARGE EGYPTIAN CAT: The Gayer-Anderson Gift. The bronze original is a votive figure of Bastet, Saite period, 600 B.C. The resin cat wears gold-plated leech-shaped earrings, nose-ring and a silver pectoral plate. Approx. 13″ high. (121R) 50-K

SPECIAL THANKS to these generous people, pussycats all: Patricia Ayres, Charles W. (Chuck) Blitzer, Ruth G. Bowen, Claudia Dombrowski, Anitra Frazier, Susan Gray, Phyllis Levy and Mimi Vang Olsen.

PHOTO CREDITS: Aaron Faber (Don Manza); Sweet Nellie (Manna Downtown); About Faces Pottery (Adam Markowitz); The Chatco Collection (T.M. Crane); Anitra Cat Grooming Plus (Terry deroy Gruber); Cat Collectors (Donald Dipboye, non-cat items); *Cat Fancy* (Robert Pearcy. Cat photos used as decoration in *The Mail-Order Cat* also by Robert Pearcy.); B. Shackman & Co. (Direct Press/Modern Litho).

 A Fireside Book, Published by Simon & Schuster, Inc., Simon & Schuster Building, Rockefeller Center, 1230 Avenue of the Americas, New York, New York 10020. FIRESIDE and colophon are registered trademarks of Simon & Schuster, Inc.

Printed in Spain by Novograph, S. A., Madrid

10 9 8 7 6 5 4 3 2 1

Library of Congress Cataloging in Publication Data

Benjamin, Alan.    The mail-order cat.

"A Fireside book."
Includes index.
1. Cats—Equipment and supplies—Catalogs.
2. Cats—Miscellanea. I. Blitzer, Barbara. II. Title.
SF447.3.B46    1985    636.8'0029'4    85-1769
ISBN 0-671-54619-8 (pbk.)

# THE MAIL-ORDER CAT

BY ALAN BENJAMIN & BARBARA BLITZER

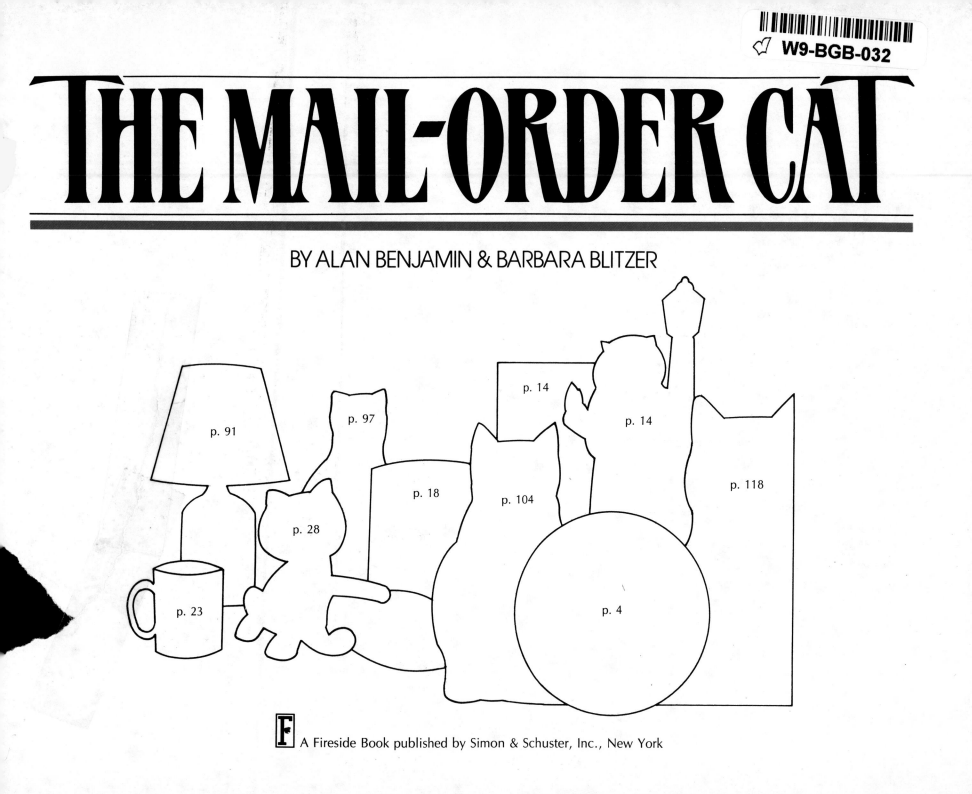

p. 91
p. 97
p. 14
p. 14
p. 18
p. 104
p. 118
p. 28
p. 23
p. 4

A Fireside Book published by Simon & Schuster, Inc., New York